Elizabeth Byrne Ferm

FREEDOM IN EDUCATION

Elizabeth Byrne Ferm

FREEDOM IN EDUCATION

Factory School

Freedom in Education by Elizabeth Byrne Ferm

Factory School, 2005

ISBN: 0-9711863-4-0

Reproduction and re-use of this work for non-commercial personal or collective purposes is permitted and encouraged. Reproduction for sale, rent or other use involving financial transaction is prohibited.

Most of this edition of Elizabeth Ferm's *Freedom in Education* is based upon the text assembled by Alexis Ferm and published in 1949 by Lear Publishers, New York. "The Spirit of Freedom" was published in the October 1917, issue of *The Modern School* magazine.

Factory School is a learning and production collective engaged in action research, multiple-media arts, publishing, and community service.

For more information, please visit: factoryschool.org

CONTENTS

1. Creative Development in Education	9
2. Educator and Child	21
3. Activity and Passivity of the Educator	25
4. License in Education	34
5. Who wins?	40
6. Limitations of Parenthood	45
7. Self-Determination in Education	49
8. Neighborhood Playhouse and Workshop	57
9. Unity in the Kindergarten	68
10. Discipline	77
11. Suggestion and Direction	81
12. Value of "Destruction" in Education	86
13. Play	94
14. Why Does the Child Play?	102
15. Rough and Tumble Play	108
16. Toys	116
17. Music in Education	122
18. Reading and Education	129
19. Adolescent Youth	133
20. Children's Emotions	143
21. Youth's Confidant	147

Appendix A:
Elizabeth Byrne Ferm – A Biographical Note
    by Alexis C. Ferm 151

Appendix B:
The Spirit of Freedom
    by Elizabeth Ferm 163

CHAPTER ONE

Creative Development in Education

If human life had been left free to reveal itself, there would be no need to consider the question of education.

Education, free from outer interference, would flow as normally through human life as the sun, moon and stars move on their way and so fulfill their use and destiny.

I am not using the word education loosely; I am using it in a definite, particular sense, i.e., as one and the same as creative evolution.

Unless an act is the outcome of an inner necessity it is not creative. If it is not creative it cannot educate. In the degree that a human expresses himself creatively, in that degree he lives. In the degree that man does not reveal himself in his daily life, in that measure he exists as a material thing and he in no way fulfills his destiny as a self-conscious being, self-determining, self-directing and self-revealing.

This point is brought out in a quotation from *Jean Christophe*: "To create physically or spiritually is to leave the prison of the human body. To create is to do that which is. To create is to kill death. Unhappy is the soul who has never felt the urge to create. The world may give the non-creative man honor and position but in so doing it crowns no living thing. It crowns a corpse. Unhappy is the soul that does not reproduce itself like a tree in flower in the springtime."

Every human being has the urge to reveal himself in his acts and he will project himself unless interfered with. Interference, no matter how it rears its head as guidance, direction, help, making the indefinite definite, etc., only serves to perplex and confuse man. Offers of help where no help is sought for, irritate and fret the child because he does not understand the why or wherefore of the intrusion into his life. When an extraneous suggestion is made to him, he cannot relate it to himself because it has no point of contact with his own development. When adults insist on blocking the individual's path by trying to focus his attention on the thing or program that they have provided to further, as they think, his growth and development, he, in self-defense, must struggle, at all and any costs, to save himself. Usually he does what everything else in the universe does, he takes the line of least resistance. I believe that, to be directed from without, to follow ways and means which are not simple and direct, obscures the individual's own impulse and results in bewilderment which, if long continued, must affect and color his whole after-life.

One of the gravest objections to our present school system is the initiation of the young into forms which have not been called out by any need or desire of the child. Herding children in child centers has made it necessary to control and regulate their activities. As the child does not understand the reason for his being gathered in with so many strange children and strange adults, one of the first problems of the teacher is how to adjust him as quickly and as pleasantly as possible into a grade or group where he seems to fit. There is no time to let the child adjust himself slowly and to find his own place.

In the school the child soon finds or senses that his acts are caused by an outer influence or permitted by an outer authority. The flow of his former life is diverted and consequently its course is no longer normal. His inner voice is stifled and though he may still feel the impulse to act independently, there are too many voices in that child center for him to distinguish his own.

From the standpoint of human growth, the outer voice is always false and totally unrelated to man's inner life. When the school succeeds in deadening the sound of the inner voice, it becomes an enemy to human development and a hindrance to life.

You probably have often seen the disastrous effect in youths and adults from regimented and supervised activities which had been devised to aid their growth. They had followed a personal leader so long, that in a crisis they were helpless without a guide, a slogan, or some outer motive to push them into action. The great danger in human life is that the artificially planned thing may so long encase the human being that he may learn to adapt himself to the artificial life.

Do you recall how Uriah Heap explained his servility? "So many Betters." That state of the individual didn't exhaust itself with Uriah. Uriah's "Betters" are still with us in the form of self-appointed custodians. I call them self-appointed because the developing human has never sought them out or attached himself to one of them. They are forced upon him and he is unlearned in ways to resist them. It is especially difficult for the child to deal with adults when reasons for the child's subjection are advanced, such as assuring him that he is an individual "whole and complete but he is also a member of a larger whole, the Social Body." The social body is like a promise of promotion. The "but" wrings the life out of wholeness and completeness. It throws the individual off his guard through its ingratiating implications.

There would be very little hope for humanity if all humans could be wheedled or forced into step and line. Here and there a rebel takes his stand and will not submit. Sometimes the conflict is so bitter and lasting that full-grown people have felt handicapped in facing a youngster who is not yet disconnected from his own center, from his own fearless inner life. Sometimes there is nothing for the adult to do but to eject the youngster from their midst. Ostracism, however, often gives the child a false sense of power and the spiritual force in his first resistance gets twisted into an outside struggle between unequal physical forces which changes its whole aspect, and may be the starting point of criminality.

I am inclined to think that, deplorable as a criminal start may be, there is more hope in it than in a submissive condition.

When the conflict between adult and young is too unequal, many children withdraw to fight the power which overawes them, evasively, shiftily. In such a relationship the young pick up a false scent which, in all likelihood, will lead them very far from their inner need, from their self-conscious base. Instead of realizing that unity was to be realized in and through individuality and diversity, they are presented with a uniformity masquerading under the name of "unity."

Uniformity is a truly barren reservation in which no living thing, no creative need can grow or manifest itself. Uniformity encloses many artificial things made to look like life, but they are only appearances of life, the result of concession, compromise and insincerity. The conforming individual is like a puppet whose every move is manipulated, the directing hand skillfully hidden from the observer. The taint of uniformity, once the virus has taken effect, seems to permeate the whole after-life.

When we observe and contemplate the surrounding world, we find an harmonious evolvement flowing from within out. This unfoldment reveals an order, a rhythm, as it flows outwardly, onwardly. The earth revolves on its own axis. The seasons have a definite order and rhythm. Days, hours, time and space reveal a unity, a correlation, a continuity which manifests their course as self-consciously directed.

In the genesis of human self-consciousness, the same order, the same rhythm flows from dark to light, from light to dark, from the universal to the particular.

> "There is no other way for light to break
> Save through the blackness of the midnight hour."

We have no method skillful enough to gauge the invisible psychic force of life. Nevertheless we psychically know that it does exist, that the psychic is more positive and compelling in our daily life than any object that we may weigh or handle physically. Personally I have found the psychic exchange with the young the simplest connecting link between us.

In the infant state we see the normal, natural development of unity manifested in the relation of mother and child, and also revealed in the infant at-one-ment with himself. In due time that unity between mother and child instinctively unfolds, and eventually is broken. That rupture causes a sense of separation. But separation is necessary to advance the individual's self-conscious development. It is the growth from instinct to mind.

I see mind and instinct as one and the same quality functioning differently but the same in essence. It is the unity realized in individuality and diversity. Instinct, I feel, leads man into the concrete world and there and then evolves a new form fitted to deal with tangible matter. This new form of instinct we now call mind because it serves a new need.

Unity, to be realized, must be proved and tested. It is not sufficient for the human, growing towards self-consciousness, to feel and enjoy a state of unity. Man is necessitated from an inner need to become conscious of it as a life basis. If instinct served man without a break, man could never attain self-knowledge.

Instinct being, as it were, the parent of the mind, knows that its offspring or offshoot is well able to face its work alone.

So it is with the child. In due time the infant reaches out to gain contact with the world surrounding him. He kicks his legs, stretches his body, yawns, smiles, sneezes and holds on to any object which is within his grasp. These visible signs indicate that there is an inner state which is gradually unfolding. There is no definite sharp line which marks the different stages of growth. The infant kicks without seeing where or what he kicks. He smiles before he observes or distinguishes things as separate and distinct from himself. *He feels himself before he knows himself.*

But even though we cannot discern that the infant recognizes anything as separate and distinct, he is not entering the outside world unprepared. He has harmoniously developed a feeling, a sense with many attributes. These attributes lend sight to his eyes, hearing to his ears, smell to his nose, taste to his tongue, feeling to his hands. These attributes, governed and directed by his sense of touch, serve the infant by going out as scouts and returning with reports which help him to face the unknown world. But this sense of touch, with its attributes, is not subject to external things. Many sounds vibrate in the infant environment which convey no message to him. Many objects pass before the infant's eyes without being recognized. Many odors are not detected by him. This exclusion of outer things reveals that the infant is not subject to things or influences external to his own inner need. He has a self-centered, self-conscious, self-determining and self-directing instinct which shuts out the useless and unnecessary things which would serve only to distract and confuse him.

The point that I am endeavoring to emphasize is, that the infant is perfectly equipped, from within, to draw in from the outside any nourishment essential to his development. Consequently we adults may free ourselves from the idea that the infant, child and youth, deprived of our wise guidance or supervision would be "up a tree." In fact, he is very much up a tree now as the result of our interference.

We have, all of us, talked more and read more about our children than we have lived *with* them. Froebel probably sensed that in his call, Come! Let us with our children live."

When a child endeavors outwardly to express an inner impulse, adults, in their eagerness to serve him, try to anticipate that need. In nine cases out of ten, they do not realize that the act is the outcome of a need for expression. The impulse is the key to the act which only the individual who tries to project the impulse, holds. Guardians of children are prone to be over-vigilant in their desire to aid and help them. Frequently the adults confuse the young, destroying the value of the impulse and its manifestations to the one who created it, because the child cannot then see himself reflected in his act. The child realizes his inner selfhood through its outer form.

It is said by those who claim to know that at no other time in the development of the human being is the rate of growth as great as it is from birth into childhood. If this is true why are adults so persistently intrusive and invasive regarding human actions?

As long as the infant is immobile and quiet, the adult has an enjoyment and interest in its manifestations of life. But as soon as the child reveals a desire to go forward to meet the objective world, the adult at once restricts and hems in the natural endeavor. In some mysterious fashion the adult, at this period of growth, develops an idea that now it is his turn and so he gets busy trying out all his theories and applying all the facts that he has held in reserve. They seem to be obsessed with the idea that they must prove their value in relation to childhood by changing the child.

Lack of development, fear or ignorance may account for the constant interference with childhood but that does not excuse it.

I firmly believe that ultimately no outside direction or control can permanently change the life of man. That belief sustains me when I feel disturbed by the methods advised to thwart life.

"Are we fools all, to sweat among the weeds
With a small plow that does not serve to turn
The smallest furrow for the need of man?"

We may verify the result of waste in education in our present chaotic state. We are "likened to the foolish man who built his house upon the shifting sand, and the rain descended and the floods came, and the wind blew and beat upon that house and it fell; and great was the fall of it."

Pedagogy, with its plan, has tried to build a house for all men, standardized for the sake of economy and utility; decorated to cover up its ugliness. From the beginning this house has cramped the individual. The stream of his life has been so blocked and hindered by the limitations it has imposed that it has left him uncertain, unsure about his own needs.

Man's sense of beauty or use is obscured by the examples set up before him. All the houses of pedagogy are uniform. But the individual's search is not for uniformity and so he is constantly bumping into corners and cubby holes that serve no purpose for him.

The individual must have a clear field in which to build his own house, fitted for his own needs; its outer form the growth of the inner need of the dweller who builds from within out.

If it is agreed that man's greatest attainment is to become self-conscious, to know himself; that every unhampered movement of man reveals the tendency toward that end and that he shares this in common with all life forms; then no one can take from nor add to man's spiritual development. The individual alone knows the way he should go. Man, accordingly, begins, at a very early age, even in infancy, to plant a firm foot on his own ground. Intuitively man feels that when he is *en rapport* with his own creative center then he is *en rapport* with the life of the universe.

Seeking for recognition and assurance from the outside is the result of previous suggestion and guidance which has left a taint of doubt and uncertainty in its wake.

The creative manifestation can be fully recognized only by the creator. No matter how well-intentioned the outer world may be in trying to help or further a creation, it is too short-sighted, in its power, to recognize its meaning. Jean Christophe tells the disappointed composer, "You did not compose for others; you wrote for yourself and God."

The creator learns through his outer rebuffs that no matter at what price, the individual alone must be the judge of the value of his creation.

The individual, developing through infancy, childhood and

youth, is spiritually sure of his direction. He is still rhythmically unfolding and flowing with the life of the universe.

Education, being in the advance guard of art, must realize that fact to become conscious of its power and freedom.

An educational relationship is allied to the most sensitive, subtle form of life. No material substance is required for its fulfillment. A conscious recognition, a psychic exchange can furnish a center. Adult and child, bound together spiritually, have every need supplied. Lacking the spiritual, every vital living thing is missing. In contrast, pedagogy must have a budget and equipment. Teachers seem to think that the material thing, the physical body, is the true approach to human life. The child is examined, tested, notes taken whereby the case may be recorded and followed up. I'm not sure that he is not finger-printed. Mentally and physically he is treated pathologically. The psychiatrist probes inwardly until it develops into a game of "cops and robbers." The psychiatrist after the individual and the individual trying to evade him.

In all accredited and approved schools adorable youngsters are subjected to great physical indignities. Once in a while a rebel turns up, refuses to submit and does what I saw a little fellow do—he runs away.

Too often, however, the parents are overawed by so much expert handling of children, so they coax or bribe the runaway into returning. The child soon learns the futility of escaping, so he appears to acquiesce. I use the word "appears" advisedly, because the human knows how to camouflage. In self-defense the child seems to submit and so throws his hunters off the scent. In such an environment every physical attribute is over-accentuated. The inner life of the human cannot be recognized in such surroundings. There is, in fact, no time for such recognition even if it is believed that an inner life does exist, for the experts in charge are already overworked.

When man creates he reveals himself outwardly in some objective form, whether in the making of a chair, a portrait, or a composition. When, however, the inner expression is in any way diverted, as in having to copy some other creation by imposition—not by self-selection, we have a thing which is not self-revealing. It has no message for anyone. It clutters the road which should be left open and free.

When the human is left free to objectify his inner life, he intuitively recognizes himself. In Froebel's words, the inner has been made outer and the outer made inner, and the two are united in life.

When, however, the individual is moved to action through an outer appeal, incentive or demand, he is unable to relate the achievement to an inner need. He must submit the accomplishment to the one who caused it to be made. It must be stamped as true or false, good or bad, by someone on the outside. Instead of seeing himself reflected in his work he does not know to whom to relate his action, because there is no meaning in it for him. One thing he does know—he has no relationship to it.

Distributing, transferring and transposing are often mistaken for spontaneous self-activity. Because one walks with his own legs from one point to another, carries things with one's own arms and hands from one place to another, the movement is often mistaken for freedom. When a restless child exhibits a tendency to break through a prescribed line the suggestion, "Wouldn't you like to do thus and so?" in order to divert him, tends to trouble the child more, mentally and psychically, than if he had been given a box on the ear. Consequently I regard the severest authority as less confusing to the captive human because it is more direct.

That is why the seductive methods of private schools are generally more dangerous to the development of free beings than the system of the public school. The public school is brutal in its frankness and therefore simple for an undeveloped human to understand. It is the nature of unspoiled humans to be direct, thus the bluntness of the public school is easily comprehended.

In the private schools the methods are, on the surface, more ingratiating and insidious, but the plans are just as firmly fixed for catching and holding the individual until they get his pattern set to their ideas of fitness, order, usefulness or beauty.

To be allowed to shuffle towards your project instead of attacking it at once and getting it finished, doesn't open any door to freedom that I care to look through.

Whether class work must be faced now or a thousand years hence is not the question. The question lies in the fact that the plan or project is from without and consequently is of no real value to man, to society or to life The very laxity, because it may be confused with freedom of choice, is more vicious in its effect on the young than the authoritative "now."

When the individual is prodded into action from without the motive seems to be to link the individual with the activities of the outer world. The connection seems to mean that he should enter the great arena and there compete and struggle with others for things and place. In the degree that the individual succumbs to these advances, in that degree he is introduced to a false estimate of values which can serve only to blunt his sense of spiritual values.

There is no uncertainty, no groping, on the part of the individual who feels himself unhampered. Every act is self-revealing, self-determined and self-directed. His absorption, when he is creative, indicates that he has something definite toward which he is moving.

No design, no example for life can be given to man. Froebel passionately declares that "no life, not even the life of Jesus, can serve as an example." Each life is particular and unique in itself. Each life must create its own form.

Einstein's belief in the one law, the one order underlying all forms of life enables him to search, watch and wait for the verification of his faith. Spiritually Einstein knows that the continuity of life manifests the one law and that in time he will be able to demonstrate it to himself and others.

Education calls for the same faith, the same belief, the same long watch and wait until the midnight blackness shall let the light break through.

We must abandon formulas, plans, projects, assignments. We must free ourselves from every artificial device no matter how subtly employed; we cannot probe into the inner life of man. When we attempt it we find ourselves before a closed door which opens only from within out. No matter how cunningly we concoct ways and means to gain an entrance there is no ingress for the outsider.

When we have developed a true respect and regard for human life, we shall have no desire to peep in or force an entrance.

CHAPTER TWO

Educator and Child

The relation between the educator and the child is a fundamental relation. No matter what changes may occur in our political, industrial, or economic states of society, the relation of the child and the educator will always be as necessary, vital and indispensable to developing human and social life as it has ever been. The relation has had and will continue to have many phases and forms, but the spirit of the relation has never changed.

The child manifests the need of an educator very early in his development. He is constantly seeking to attach himself to adult life. The child intuitively turns to adults for the corroboration, connection and relation of the past to the present. Instinctively, he feels those strivings, aspirations and achievements of the race which the adult understands. In his simple direct way, he turns to adult life for assurance, recognition and interpretation of human life.

The child expects to find the experiences which have preceded his advent summed up as self-knowledge in the life of the adult. When the child learns that age necessarily does not develop consciousness; that age is often less in touch with the real experiences of life than youth and childhood; that adult life has rarely any understanding of even its own physical need, the child becomes a reactionary and treats adulthood shabbily.

The child is then inconsiderate, disrespectful. He instinctively expresses contempt for the human who has accumulated wrinkles without thought, failing eyes that have never had a vision, deaf ears that have never heard the message of life. The child is intuitively repelled.

When, however, the child finds himself in conjunction with self-conscious adult life, he inwardly unfolds and develops by leaps and bounds. There is mutual recognition and mutual assurance. The impulses and instincts of the child are verified in the life of the self-conscious adult. Such an adult the child selects as an educator. The child clings to such an adult as a vine clings to an oak. Such an adult is able to interpret to the child the life which the young are facing. In the degree that the adult understands and relates the experiences of his own life, he can in that degree aid and help the developing child in his adventure.

When I use the term educator I trust it will not be confused with that of teacher, and when I refer to education that it will not be confounded with pedagogy.

I am not putting new wine into old bottles when I separate education from pedagogy. The pedagogues are the offenders. They usurped the title. Education and teaching are terms so loosely used that many think of them as interchangeable.

Education may include pedagogy, as, for example, when a child asks for a point of information. But pedagogy cannot and does not include education.

Education is that which has to do with unfolding, revealing and making concrete the inner life, the spiritual life of the individual. That which gives opportunity for the development of the real self in man; that which enables the individual to realize himself physically, mentally and spiritually, as an entity, as a complete whole, is educational.

The educator is one who understands the law underlying the instinct, impulse and desire of the child; one who is able to clarify for the child the forces that move the child to action. The educator is an adult who knows—through his own experiences—that within and above the human endeavor, no matter how offensive its expression may be, there is the effort of the real, the true self to express itself in the external.

The educator is the very antithesis of the pedagogue. The educator deals with and integrates for the child his present experience; the relation of the present moment, present hour and present day to the child's life.

The educator may refer to the past and future to confirm the present experience of the child and to reveal the continuity of the spirit of life to the child; but never in true education is the past or the future allowed to obscure, influence or govern the now, the here of the child's daily experiences.

The educator may supply a very simple need of the child. He may be the story-teller of the neighborhood. Through the story the adult is able to give the child the history of the spiritual development of the race. The story—to have any real value—must be free from intention to mold or influence the action of the child. It must reveal without moralizing. Children despise stories told with an obvious purpose. I am inclined to think they resent it as a rebuke to their own expression.

I recall how children corrected me in my early kindergarten days, when I attempted to influence their lives by holding before them ideal types of humanity. A boy confided to me that he was going "to get even" with another "fellow," who had played a mean trick on him.

I stupidly interposed, "Do you think the Christ child would do that?"

The boy's face flushed and he impatiently answered, "What do I care about the Christ child? He must have been a funny fellow if he never had a fight."

That rebuke opened my eyes a wee bit. I never made that ignorant blunder again.

On another occasion I experimented with a boy and he verified the first boy's position. This boy's mother was a Salvation Army woman. The boy was constantly talking over the religious questions he heard at his home. One day he came to the kindergarten in a very excited state. He said he was going to get a pistol from his uncle, so that he could shoot some boys who wanted to fight him. I said, "Well, Paul, I can't understand how you could shoot at anyone. Didn't Jesus say you must turn the other cheek, and if anyone takes you one mile you must go three?"

The boy gave me a surprised look and said, "That would be foolish! They'd kill you! This is what you should do: hit them first and then turn the other cheek."

Education cannot be reduced to a system. It cannot be standardized. There is no method for demonstrating its efficiency. Every locality must reveal its educational need in a particular manner. Education is a spiritual union of unconscious youth and conscious age. No degree can make an educator. The spiritual development of adult life is the magnet which attracts and holds the developing child. The bond is an inner one.

The fresh impulse of life which the young reveal should confirm the experiences of age and give it a new impetus to life. In exchange age should be able to recognize and assure the child that the "open road" which beckons to him, is safe and sure, though full of adventure.

Educator and child are interdependent and mutually necessary to each other.

"To educate one's self and others, with consciousness, freedom and self-determination is a two-fold achievement of wisdom. It began with the first appearance of man upon the earth; it was manifested with the first appearance of full self-consciousness in man; it begins now to proclaim itself as a necessary requirement of humanity; and to be heard and heeded as such."

CHAPTER THREE

Activity and Passivity of the Educator

There are two important qualities of the true educator: activity and passivity. If I were asked which attribute I considered the greater, I would unhesitatingly say passivity.

Do not confuse inability to control a situation—neglect to seize the moment—indifference to the outcome—timidity of action—or any other form of weakness, with passivity.

Passivity, as I conceive it, is a conscious keeping off of hands, a deliberate letting alone. There is no passivity unless the educator has an understanding of the particular child whom he is striving to educate, unless he can recognize and follow the purpose and outcome of that particular child's acts.

The professed friends and believers in passivity are often the ones who discredit it and hold it up to ridicule.

I once visited the home of a friend who was the mother of two children. The flat irons were left on the floor, so the children, almost every day, would fit their feet into them and slide along the highly polished, waxed floors. The father and mother were distressed by the noise they made and by the damage to the floors. They would take no action, however, because they had committed themselves to the idea of passivity in education. I suggested that the rational thing to do was to put the flat irons in the cupboard or on a shelf. If the children showed by word or deed that the flat irons were a positive need in their development, then they might with some reasonableness take them out again. The children were using them as they would any old thing which might be lying about.

On another occasion I called at the home of a woman who edited and published an educational magazine. She was another victim of the idea of passivity. She had sent for me. She was distracted. The coffee-mill had been negligently left on the sitting-room table. When I put in an appearance the coffee beans were scattered over the rug and the coffee mill was thrown to one side. The child seemed to have no further use for nor interest in them. He was tugging and pulling at other subjects in the room. The mother was lying on the couch, overcome—as she phrased it—by the state of things. Instead of being overcome by the situation, she was too negative, too weak to deal with it. She was on the verge of hysterics and kept on assuring me that she didn't want me to do anything but just sit with her.

I told her I would sit with her after I had put the coffee mill in its place and brushed up the coffee beans. She wondered if it would interfere with the child's development if the coffee-mill were put away. I took it upon myself to assure her that he was too busy to miss it and that I did not believe he would pine after it.

In everything that has to do with the individual's inner life—with self-expression—the educator should follow the child.

The educator may commend the child's self-expression, but may not condemn it; may recognize his self-expression, but may not criticize it; may encourage the child's self-expression, but may not interfere with it. (This relates to the creative instinct.)

Such a relation between child and adult calls out and fosters the creative power of the individual, a power latent in all human beings. Such an attitude calls for a wide and deep understanding.

It is easy enough to follow the child passively as long as his expressions are agreeable to the educator and in no way clash with the preconceived ideas and sensibilities of the adult. But to be able to recognize that every act of the child is necessitated from within is extremely difficult. And yet, every true and earnest educator knows even when he fails to practice it, that the safest and sanest thing is to let the child do the thing he wishes, and then let him reap the harvest he has sown.

This does not mean allowing the child to jump from the Empire State Building, to fall from a precipice or to be run over. If a child should thoughtlessly or willfully place himself in a dangerous position, the human as well as the rational thing to do would be to save the child from serious consequences. I simply mean that the child should be allowed to endure all that he is capable of enduring. He should face all that he has intentionally or unintentionally created, excited or provoked.

Letting alone may look like passivity. Non-interference may look like passivity. But to my mind there is no true passivity unless the educator is consciously striving to aid the child to attain knowledge of himself through and by means of the child's own acts and experiences.

Permitting the child to do the things he desires because the adults feels that the child has the right, as an individual, to do it, is not the passivity of the educator. Permitting the child to do what he wants is the relation of individual to individual. The educator's relation is more interior than that.

In education the child must be allowed to do the thing he wants to do, because he should have the right to do it, plus the understanding of why he wants to do it; why he is so actuated.

Many years of experience with children have forced me to the conclusion that before the relation of adult and child can become an educational one, it must be psychically established. And I know of no material agency by which the psychic is demonstrated to the child's consciousness—which I allow is wholly physical—unless you will concede that the tone of the voice, the stroke of the hand, the expression of the face are palpable, tangible means by which the inner relation may manifest itself. Whether your mind can or cannot concede that such a relation is fundamental to education, I still maintain that the psychic quality must exist in order to make the relation real and enduring, fitted to weather the storm and stress of their association, as child and educator.

Because of the psychic bond the educator can have order restored out of the most chaotic condition. Our doubting friends may insist that there must be something in the attitude of the educator, something physical to overrule a disorderly state. Well, let them experiment with young children and watch the result.

Have you ever tried to affect a loving manner towards children when you were internally disturbed and wholly out of touch with them? Or have you assumed a commanding attitude when there was neither ability nor power to maintain the position? If you have, you also remember how you tried to wheedle the child, by soft words and simulated smiles, into complying—without success—and how, in the other case you blustered and fumed, and the child remained fixed, unchanged.

Children, like all simple, undeveloped natures, have a way of exposing sham. They are not mentally sophisticated enough to imagine what may or may not happen to them if they refuse to yield. They deal with the actual situation which, when such methods are used, is essentially weak and untenable.

On the other hand, if the educator is *at one*—spiritually—with the child, the most discordant condition can be changed into one that is peaceful, by the child himself.

For example, one child may, through his general interference with the activities of others, create an uproar which is difficult to control. The excitement is too great to get down to the initial cause. Whatever incident started the commotion, the tumult makes it impossible to find out. The thing for the educator to recognize is that they are out of relation with one another. They are decentralized as individuals. The educator must help them to regain consciousness of themselves and the consciousness of their association to one another.

As an illustration, take a room which has fifteen or twenty children in it. They are all busy doing things in their different ways. So many activities create a great deal of noise. One boy is sliding a chair along the floor. He does not see another boy, who has just stepped forward. In a second there is a collision. According to his temperament the boy who has been struck may either cry or try to strike the other child. The misunderstanding develops into a grievance; other children are involved. Friends become enemies. The strong and brave fight out their claim; the weaker ones vent their feelings by spitting, making faces at one another and calling names. The mob rules: Something must be done to restore a free condition, in which all may have a chance to express themselves. What shall that something be? Punish the aggressive ones? Become one of the mob also? Hardly! The needed thing is for the educator to realize what elements are lacking in that human gathering and try to restore them by calling them out of the children. The children are scattered mentally. Their human association is upset. They are simply reflecting their own disturbed states to one another.

Now is the time for the educator to summon to the rescue all the composure of spirit that he possesses. His inner serenity must be shown outwardly. Tranquil where the child is agitated; quiet where the child is noisy. When the educator is well centered within, he creates an atmosphere in which all begin to breathe and live as human beings. In less time than it takes to tell it, the mob has quelled itself and peace is restored. Once more a free society is established. The children feel the situation, but they do not understand it; they are contrite and ashamed of themselves. This result has been evolved from the inner attitude of the educator and the inner response of the children.

Such experiences cannot be trumped up. They are true indicators of the soundness of the educational relation.

After such an occurrence there is always a deeper and more sympathetic relation. They have struggled through something. They have sounded the depths in one another. They have touched bottom. They have had an experience together. They have had a realization together. *They feel the unity of human life.*

I have especially dwelt on the passivity of the educator, because it is the most difficult relation for educators generally, and because it is particularly so for myself. It is well known that we attribute the highest quality to the thing of which we possess the least. Let me once more emphasize that the passivity of the educator has to do with all that relates to individual self-expression, self-activity.

The *activity* of the educator must be objectified by the educator becoming a creative, self-active member of the little society in which he finds himself as an individual. And also, through the consciousness with which he is able to reveal and reflect the social basis upon which we must all stand. The child is ignorant of any law or principle which binds or relates him to his playmate. When he finds himself in a trying situation with another child—whom he is not able to thrash or intimidate—he will suggest a compromise or will make a concession himself, which will put him in possession of the thing that he is after.

The child's understanding of things is proportioned to his experiences. He is very jealous about his own rights, his own possessions. *He senses might as right.* He does not scruple to encroach upon the rights of others, to carry off their belongings. Although he resents any invasion of his rights, he does not know how to maintain a position against such trespassing.

The educator, understanding why the child is actuated to leave his home, why he is actuated to develop a social relation with others, must emphasize the principles which unite all forms of human association.

I believe the child leaves his home to find himself as an individual. To know himself as an individual, he must intermingle with other individuals. The condition for such an experience must be founded on equality and equity. To realize equality and equity, he must have the conditions which will objectify those principles.

The child's natural opportunity, for instance, may consist of space, chairs, tables, materials to work with; everything in the place to be considered as common property; all having equal share; all having equal responsibilities.

Zealously and jealously these opportunities are watched by the educator; the principle of equality and equity is to be called out through their use. For instance, a child finds that he is the first arrival in the morning. He looks about him and naturally concludes that his right is bounded only by the limitations of the place. He may use, as he chooses, the opportunities which the place offers. He starts a line of cars, which takes in every chair in the room. Another child enters. The newcomer may not allow himself to think that he has any claim to a chair, because he sees them all utilized. The educator knows, however, that before long that utilization will change into monopoly and then a conflict will ensue. Another child arrives. The chair suggests a train to him. He demands some of the chairs, or he attempts to take them. The one in possession in great wrath defends his property and beats off the newcomer. If the monopolizer is physically strong enough to keep the new claimant off, he will, possibly, be left in control.

This is a situation that calls for the activity of the educator.

"Philip, why did Jakey hit you?"

"I wanted some chairs."

"Did you ask Jakey for them?"

"No! I took one."

"Perhaps Jakey does not understand you. Go and tell Jakey that you want some of the chairs."

Philip goes to Jakey but Jakey is watching things now. He is so inflated by his former success that he answers Philip with a blow. Philip does not feel like insisting on getting chairs, and is about to give up. Now is the educator's chance to emphasize Philip's right, as against Jakey's might.

"Jakey, why are you not willing to let Philip have some chairs?"

"I had them first. I want to use them," is the reply.

Jakey is told that he has the right to use everything in the room as long as no one else wishes to share it. But as soon as Philip feels that he, too, wishes to make a train of cars with the chairs, Jakey can no longer keep all of them.

Sometimes the dispute may arise over the use of something—say a swing—of which there is only one. A certain child may like it more than others, or want to control it and prevent the others from using it. A complaint is made that Sarah won't let Gussie swing. After Sarah has given her reasons—which usually go back to the fact that she was there first and she has not finished using it—Sarah is told that the others are not obliged to wait for her will and pleasure. The way to be fair to one another, when there is only one swing and others desire to have a chance, is for them to come to some agreement as to how long each one shall use it; the mere getting of a thing first does not give one the right to dominate it. Sarah is told that she must relinquish the swing, if she is not willing to use it with the others. If Sarah refuses to share the swing, she must be put off.

The simple, crude, physical consciousness conceives success as the just, the *right* cause. Success excites admiration; it indicates power. And power is the greatest thing that the physical consciousness can comprehend. Power to the simple mind implies life. Defeat, on the other hand, produces the opposite effect. It suggests weakness and weakness implies death. There is no tangible way of demonstrating the right of a thing, if it is followed by non-success. It may call out pity but the cause is questioned. It arouses fear and mistrust. The physical consciousness is afraid of being involved in it. The cause is finally deserted. The educator, knowing this fact, must be careful in objectifying a principle in such a manner that the simple state of the child's mind may be able to entertain it. The child is instinctively right when he unites himself with the successful side and shrinks from the defeated cause.

Success *should* follow that which is true and just; what is false and wrong *should* suffer defeat.

I sometimes think that the reason why success does not follow the right is in a great measure due to our early impressions and conclusions. For instance, a strong child has usurped the place of a weaker one. The weaker one tearfully submits, or, at the most, he may try to kick the usurper. There seems to be no idea in their minds that there is any *right*. Everything is measured by might. The educator must take an active part in such an experience. An indignant protest from the educator against the physical domination on the one hand, and the meek submission on the other, will have its effect. Tyrant and slave are equally astonished. They have never heard the submissive one reproached before. The yielding child has never been treated before as a social offender. The educator insists that the right thing for the submissive one is to resume and keep the place which the tyrant usurped from him. This attitude creates a new order of things. A revolution takes place in custom and thought. Right enthroned, might dethroned. The one who maintains and defends the new order is recognized as the strongest one in the room. Strength—not used to subjugate the weak, but to help the weak to become strong in action, and the physically strong to develop a more honorable and human relation to their playmates.

In everything that has to do with the social experiences of the child, the educator is actively leading. The educator may be the only one in the group who has had social experiences. And as our idea of equality and fairness was evolved from our social experiences, the child knows nothing of them. He has had no social experiences. The idea of justice does not have to be imposed on the child; he responds to it and holds himself close to the condition or place in which it is accentuated.

CHAPTER FOUR

License in Education

In the present struggle for greater freedom of opportunity for the child, there is no greater stumbling block to its realization than the championship it receives from, those who hold abstract idealistic conceptions of life and freedom.

Freedom they conceive as a spiral of ascending joy and peace, based upon an environment devoid of all that is harsh and ugly. They encircle the developing child with flowers and sculpture, pictures, music and literature, which are calculated to influence the child's life and mold his character.

The consternation of such well-meaning people, when they find the child repudiating their esthetically prescribed surrounding and creating in its stead an environment of his own, in which he is able to balance his life through struggle and peace, through pain and joy, reveals how unstable and limited their outlook on real life is. They refuse to accept growth which develops through turmoil and friction and pain.

"This is license," they exclaim. "License is not freedom."

Fearfully they gather their strings about the child again—strings which they had never discarded, but only allowed to slacken in their grasp and firmly and determinedly they draw the child back into their gilded cage, where they strive to allure the child into a make-believe life, a make-believe world and a make-believe freedom.

A kindergartner answered my plea for greater freedom for the child by saying, "I tried freedom for one morning. That was enough for me."

As physical freedom simply means opportunity for self-expression, and as life in its endeavor to express itself creates struggle and pain, it is folly to expect only joy, happiness and peace from a free condition or state. Joy is always balanced by pain. Freedom has its bitter and its sweet.

In the primitive conception of life, which the child holds, we find the child, when unrestrained, vigorously manifesting his desires. In his aggressiveness, we find the natural crudity of every initial effort.

When license rears its head in a free association, there is no need to sound an alarm against freedom. The cause of license lies in the limited conception of freedom which the child holds. License is the lowest rung in the ladder of freedom, but we must remember that it is an indispensable rung, which developing man must use in his ascent to fuller and nobler living.

License indicates that desire is not balanced by a sense of values and proportion. License is freedom in the rough, disguised in an uncouth, unpolished form. In its essence, however, it is one and the same as the freedom which we all crave and endeavor to establish. Human association—in the free relation—will speedily remove the rough edges from the early manifestations of freedom.

The child's experience with other humans will, in the order of time, develop his sense of value. To restrict an expression because license is taken betrays a lack of human development—on the part of adults—which equals if it does not exceed that of the child, who conceived license as full and perfect freedom.

Freedom has as many attributes and phases as any other quality in man's consciousness. It cannot be grasped and measured as a static fixed thing. It is always relative to man's state of consciousness and stage of development. It is so dynamic in its quality and force, it becomes elusive, as soon as the individual tries to organize or embody it.

The individual strives to realize freedom in some fixed way, only to find that the way is the path of bondage. All forms of life—whether inorganic or organic—reveal the struggle to be free. But each expresses it differently, showing us that forms of freedom must be as manifold and as fluid as life itself. Man must free himself. And he must attain it through his own development and consciousness.

As A. E. puts it, "Freedom is a virtue of the soul." The only aid, therefore, that adults can give the child in his struggle for freedom is to recognize it as a dynamic force in life, justified by its persistent, insistent and uncontrollable quality.

There is no process for developing freedom; it is in itself a process of development. Free man evolves from youth; free youth from free childhood; free childhood from free infanthood; and free infanthood from free conditions.

We may have ideas of freedom without experiencing any phase of freedom, but there can be no real consciousness or knowledge of the quality of freedom which does not come to us through our own experiences in life.

Our experiences are the result of our conceptions; our conceptions are the result of our impressions; our impressions are the result of our sensations; and our sensations are produced by actual contact with the life and things surrounding us. Such is the law and the order of development.

An infant restricted from free physical movement must carry over into his next physical stage of development, i.e., the child stage, the expressions which naturally belonged to his infant stage. The fettered expression of one stage of development must be carried over and worked out in another stage. Expressions of infancy in childhood are out of relation. When a thing is out of relation its proportions and true worth are lost.

When an adult acts like a youth, when a youth acts like a child, when a child acts like an infant, the act becomes either silly or repulsive. When, however, an adult conjoins the simple directness of childhood with his mature physical and mental development, his life is rounded and full indeed; but when we find an adult with a consciousness belonging to childhood, we find a stunted, dwarfed development.

In the child's attempt to understand his own life he measures it against the life which surrounds him, by hindering, thwarting and intercepting the progress of the form of life which attracts his attention. If the child sees a fly he may try to catch it. If another child is running past him, he may try to stop the child by catching or tripping him. Such displays of power belong to a child's early development.

When we find grown-ups gauging their power by blocking the progress of others, we may be quite sure that they are exhibiting a state which belonged to an earlier period of development. Every form of exploitation and monopoly is rooted in the same crudity of thought, i.e., that the success of one is attained through another's defeat. The harsh expression of the child—with his limited power to inflict suffering—affects all thoughtful adults disagreeably. We are tempted to divert his interest or influence his act so that his victim may escape him; but when we see indifferent grown-ups inflated with a sense of personal power and greatness through hindering the life expression of animals and humans, we are repelled from such expressions as unworthy of adult life.

If such manifestations expressed true adult development we might despair indeed. But when we see it as the result of earlier influences—which prevented a normal expression—we realize that while we are powerless to undo the evil effect of the past, we can stop perpetuating the conditions which create and foster the evil.

We cannot change grown-ups, but we can save the young by removing the bars which obstruct the natural expressions of humanity. Every life is "particular and unique in itself." Let us cease trying to shape and model it.

Every infant born into the world is the herald of the instinct, impulse and spirit of freedom. It manifests itself in every infant like a new-born effort in the life of humanity.

The infant reveals no heredity of repression or restraint. He comes into the world with an unhampered, unharnessed spirit. He cannot be diverted from his need. No form of cajolery, argument or punishment can alter his set purpose. The infant is free from all the social weapons, i.e., shame and fear. Even physical suffering cannot subdue him. The more punishment you inflict the louder he screams. The history of every conflict with infanthood spells defeat for the adult. The infant rules the household. Every adult—in the infant's kingdom, for that is what it resolves itself into—is a subject during the period of infancy.

The infant is the dominant tone because he is the only free spirit in the home. The struggle between the free spirit of infanthood and the bond-spirit of adulthood must result in victory for the infant. There is no instinct shown in infanthood of domination or control over adult life. The struggle is invited by the adults who supervise and care for the infant. Adults usually greet the infant's entrance upon life with rules and regulations which, when they attempt to impose them on the infant, create opposition. Out of the conflict we find the unconquerable spirit of the infant triumphant and free and the bond spirit of the adults who strove to conquer, vanquished and subjected.

Even on the threshold of child life we find the same impulse of freedom expressed. The child wants to do everything for himself. He wants to dress himself, go up and down stairs alone, get his own chair, etc. With his physical growth, however, he has also developed a discriminating sense which separates and divides the homogeneous and indivisible life of his infant state. The child with his new development of consciousness, is reaching out toward the external. Outside things attract him. He strives to attain them. He soon realizes, however, that the outer things are claimed and controlled by adults, who guard them.

The child desires to possess the thing which attracts his attention. He is impelled by his inner need, to test and prove the quality of the things which surround him. The child soon learns that the outer world is one of privilege and monopoly. The child must bargain and barter with adults if he is to gain his end. "If you are a good boy"—which usually means being negative and submissive—"you may have it." "If you promise mother not to annoy her," etc.

The child is soon caught in the net which will land him a long way from his former free state. The lure of things—which he sees spread before him—entices him on. He cannot retrace his steps, for he does not know by which path he came. Now adults become victorious and the child is vanquished. The inner life of the infant is subordinated to the other thing.

I often ask myself if this surrender is inevitable. Is it involved in the process of human development? Can we avoid the subjugation of the inner life to outer things? Are interfering adults necessary as infanthood merges into childhood? Can we imagine a spontaneous, self-active, self-developing human making progress, continuously, through all the different stages of his development?

I believe that we can do more than imagine such a condition. We have it in our power to realize such a state if we are determined to strive for it.

The greatest understanding attainable by the individual is in knowing himself as a creative being.

Man's contribution and value to society lies in how he has revealed his inner life in his external surroundings, and not by the influence he exerted on the lives of other humans.

CHAPTER FIVE

Who Wins?

I used to think that after the triumphant sovereignty of infancy the grown-up held the reins of power. After greater observation and experience I have come to the conclusion that the adult, when he engages in a conflict with the young, is never victorious—whether it is with infancy, childhood or youth.

Life would seem like a huge joke if youth were subject to age. Physically the struggle between them is like that of life with death. Mentally it is the conflict between the dynamic and the static. Spiritually it is the struggle between creative spirit and established form. The struggle is unending. It has always existed and will continue to exist. It is the disturbance involved in all change and growth.

Parent Groups and Teacher Groups meet in conclave with experts to direct and guide them. Dogmatic psychologists attempt to extend to these study groups the technique which will enable them to deal scientifically with the problem of the young. Formulas are passed on which never operate effectively. The singular personality of each individual, the special contribution of each child is unforeseen, unknown, and therefore cannot be calculated or measured.

These conferences remind me of the painting "The Ascension of the Virgin," which depicts how insensitive the churchmen were to the spiritual truths which they were supposed to protect. While they were disputing the question, the ascension of the Spirit took place. Angelic messengers flew around the churchmen, but they were oblivious to their presence. Far removed from the tomb stood a poet entranced by the vision of the spiritual ascension.

And so we perceive in our own day that patterns for life in these study groups are so precisely presented to the adults that they are overawed. The less they understand the meaning of the curriculum, the less doubt they entertain. They are diverted from finding out that the real problem is not the child, but the attitude of the adult towards the child.

A well-known psychologist, who never doubted the result of her analysis, whether the subject was young or old, one day, when on her "analytic" rounds, called on one of her student's mothers. The boy, a sturdy chap of five, insisted on staying right in the room where his mother entertained the visitor. The mother was embarrassed because she did not understand the boy's unusual attitude. Presently, the analyst pointed to the quiet, attentive boy and announced with authority, "Now, what that boy needs is to play," when as a matter of fact the mother knew that the boy was always playing. Very like the churchmen and the Ascension.

When we try to fit the life expressions of the child for group study, we discover that life is absent and the subjects considered become unrelated acts and conduct removed from the state and time in which they happen. Life reveals itself through self-expression. The more you attempt to diagnose self-expression, the less you seem to understand it. If self-expression discloses nothing to you, then no amount of analysis will help. When adults recognize the value of the creative life to the young, they in some degree ally themselves with the young. Through that recognition youth and age are united. That recognition, however, does not entitle age to lead youth. It extends to age the privilege to follow behind, and if they have the capacity they may rejoice in youth's audacious adventures. Mishaps on the way, perhaps, but youth is not deterred by danger. Youth faces difficulties by contracting, expanding and bending itself before them.

I remember an incident when I visited a friend who is the mother of four handsome girls. The youngest one had just come home from school. When I entered, mother and daughter looked flushed and disturbed. The girl, about ten years of age, was too engrossed with her own affairs to notice me. She held a little doll in her arms. She had evidently changed her frock, because the mother very positively told her that she should take it off. I tried to act as if I were not aware of any trouble. I endeavored to speak with my friend concerning the reason for my visit. The mother tried to interest herself, but she was just as upset as her daughter. Finally she blurted out the story. Florence had been invited to a doll's party that afternoon. My friend did not approve. She maintained that when Florence came from school she required rest and quiet. My friend thought that the mother who was giving the party was very designing. Having an only child, she was glad to have an excuse to assemble other children so that her Elmira would be less exacting and irritable. Consequently, she was repeatedly making attractive proposals to get the neighborhood children to her home.

Florence was watching her mother very closely and, instinctively, I thought, felt her mother was clearing the way by talking it out. When Florence heard us discussing something alien to her needs or wants, she noisily threw herself on the couch and grunted. I decided I had better leave because the mother was too much affected by Florence's conduct. But suddenly the mother turned to Florence and said, "Well, you may go, but remember, you are to leave at five o'clock."

Florence grabbed her hat and coat, (she still wore the frock she had been told to change), took her doll from the couch and was about to dash out when her mother asked, "How will you know when it is five o'clock?"

Florence answered, "I don't know." After an awkward pause, Florence naively added, "I'll leave when it is dark," which would have been about seven p. m. My friend seemed relieved to have the struggle ended, but she did not look very triumphant. She eased her mind by blaming the neighbor.

It was interesting to me to see how she tried to save some vestige of authority by making the time stipulation. How cleverly the daughter took advantage of the concession and hurried up to be in time for the party! The loss to Florence was the time lost in the personal conflict. Well, if the party started without Florence, she would be there for the close anyway. What a true feeling for the value of time Florence showed! Time wasted at one end elastically stretched out at the other. The young are not hampered by abstract ideas of time. What they can do with it is their only concern. I appreciated the mother's plight, but my sympathy and interest were with the youngster. Why should the tired, jaded nerves of age prescribe rest and quiet for the young? In all my experience I have not met a self-active child who needed rest and quiet during the day. I have seen children irritated, excited, infuriated and exhausted from impotent rage when their self-expression, self-activity was frustrated. I have heard mothers, when they were embarrassed by such displays, interpret these exhibitions as need for a nap. We accept such explanations as excuses.

I recall the struggle of a three-year-old boy who had been invited to get his chair to eat supper with some friends in the dining room. He tried to haul and pull his chair from the kitchen, but with rugs and furniture in the way it was not an easy job. Besides, the kitchen and dining rooms were not adjoining rooms. The mother, amused at his effort, picked up the chair to carry it for him. The little fellow screamed and threw himself on the floor. When the mother tried to pacify him, he kicked her and would not allow her to approach him. It finally dawned on someone present that Eugene wanted to get the chair to the dining room himself. The chair was brought back and placed beside him. He was left alone. In a very short time Eugene was on his feet and resumed the struggle of getting the chair to the dining room, which he succeeded in doing. The tear stains and dirt marks on his face were the only signs left of the struggle. The mother was the one who suffered. She was the one who needed the rest and quiet. Eugene, flushed with the achievement, mounted his chair and ate his meal with his friends as if nothing had happened to disturb him.

The modern mother is torn between feelings and ideas. Feelings pull her one way, ideas steer her in another direction. The modern methods are dogmatic, and exacting on parent, teacher and child. The remedies recommended by psychologists do not always fit. A mother told me that she never found any of them a help, because her boy never acted in a manner for her to apply the remedy.

When young and old are unhampered in their relation with one another, they will act very much like Eugene with his chair. They will resume doing the thing from which they were sidetracked. The dreaded analyses, tests, suggestions and hindrances will be thrown into the discard along with other exploded cure-alls.

CHAPTER SIX

Limitations of Parenthood

The natural and consequently the most beneficial period of Parenthood is that which is expressed and lived out in the nursery.

The parents, during the child's infancy, instinctively subordinate every personal interest, every personal feeling, to minister to the child's needs. Their sheltering care fosters and protects the life of the child. The child is the only truly living and developing one in the circle. The household is subservient to him. The child reigns. The child is supreme.

The parents, during that period, try to develop those faculties and qualities which best serve the whole being of the child.

You may well question the beauty in such a subordinate state! Then question the beauty of the petals as they surround and protect the seed-flower.

Froebel has expressed this state when he says: "That which the life of the child requireth, the mother's heart alike desireth."

Of course, there are as many phases in the nursery life as there are phases of development in the humans who become parents.

A few men and women are conscious of what is entailed in parenthood. They realize its function. They recognize their subordinate position and do not rebel.

On the other hand we find men and women *involved* in parenthood, unprepared, unfitted, by their own tumultuous and undeveloped natures, to give the child the safe and secure environment which the nursery period demands.

Such parents *fight with* their young and *fight for* their young.

Peer Gynt's mother is a type of that stage of development.

But the child, during that period—whether his environment is consciously or unconsciously made, rules the situation and controls the environment. His needs come first.

If men and women, in and through their parenthood, developed an individual sanity along with the individual development of the child, there would be no limitation or shortcoming for us to consider or feel anxious about. But because there comes a time in the child's life when he must leave the sheltered relation and face the world as an individual, the nursery period comes to an end. The relation of parent and child is changed.

Sometimes we may say with Browning:

> "Nothing can be as it has been before;
> Better, so call it, only not the same.
> To draw one beauty into our hearts' core,
> And keep it changeless! such our claim;
> So answered—Never more!"

But more often we have to record the relation ended. Nothing evolved from it. Nothing to base any further relation upon. Parents insist on being parents to an individual. This is their great limitation.

The individual must experience the democratic life of human beings. He is impelled by the law of his development to go out to associate with other humans on equal terms. The social impulse urges him on. The child, reluctantly, dethrones himself and obeys the insistent human call.

How is this need of the individual child met by the parents? With fear and distrust.

Let their child throw himself into that human crucible called the world, on common terms, without their protection and intervention? Not at all! Are they not his parents?

They refuse to recognize that the nursling has developed beyond the nursing stage. Often in their anxiety they go out ahead of the child as emissaries to negotiate for privilege and place for their offspring. If the child's adventure is just to play on the street the other children are cajoled or bribed into holding a position with their child which has not been earned. If he goes to the kindergarten, they are satisfied only when they have seen him leading in every game. When he goes to school, they flatter the teacher with favors or they bribe their child with gifts to induce him to carry off the prizes.

When he goes into the commercial world, they scurry about to have their influence work to his advantage. Everything is done to prevent their offspring from realizing his own ability, his own strength. Parents carry their obsession to such an extreme that they endeavor to extend their protection beyond the grave by insuring their lives for his benefit.

It is not surprising to find individuals seeking "easy money" when they have to forage for themselves. That has been their preparation in the majority of homes.

The spiritual urge which compels the individual to go out to face life unprotected is frustrated by the limitations of his parents. In such an environment he cannot find himself as a human. The inner need of his life is exploited for some outward thing. He hears the unscrupulous bargaining and sees the unscrupulous actions toward society for his material and physical advantage.

His parents are concerned about every outer thing of his life but fail to recognize his real or true need.

Parents equip their children with a politician's outfit. By example they teach him how to concede, compromise, bribe and buy his way through society. How many men and women can testify to any true inner relation with their parents?

Individuals have thought themselves fortunate if their physical needs have been understood by their parents, but to have an inner need sympathized with, a need that might disturb the child's physical security, was never given to anyone whom I have known.

Parents should learn to discriminate between an infant need and an individual need. They should be able to see their child cross the threshold of their home as a potential individual striving to see himself reflected in his acts and also striving to find his image in the likeness of his playmate. When a free child returns to his home he has something to contribute to the home and in the contribution the lives of his parents are broadened, enlarged.

Instead of fearfully searching to protect their young, they will be free to widen their own interests and share with their child the experiences which his going out, unprotected, invited to him.

CHAPTER SEVEN

Self-Determination in Education

Froebel said, "Whoever is to do with self-determination and freedom that which is divine and eternal, must be at liberty to do that which is earthly and finite."

In theory the value of self-determination is rarely disputed. But when we face the practical demands of self-determination in education, differences arise which create opposition and antagonism.

After many years of practical kindergarten work, we realized that the kindergarten system did not serve to help the child to develop as an individual. Froebel's educational principles we fully agreed with, because they were verified in the life of the child; but we found that his system, like all systems, hindered the very thing that Froebel most desired to help the child to realize, i.e., self-consciousness through "spontaneous self-activity."

Nature insists that the individual shall develop according to the law of his own being. Systems are intended to guide and control the expressions of humans.

System rests on rule. Development rests on law!

After we were fully convinced that the fascinating kindergarten system, with its artful devices, and the simple crude consciousness of the child did not fit into one another, we concluded that if we were ever to get at the real need of child life, we should turn to the child and let him reveal to us his true nature and allow him to lead us into an understanding of what was best for him.

This sounds very pretty on paper, but I assure you there was nothing pretty about the actuality. The highly dramatized and esthetic plays of the kindergarten were driven out of doors by the children, and in came a roaring lusty life to which we hardly knew how to adapt ourselves. Each child accepted the free condition as his right, and proceeded to live in it. We probably felt we were conferring a privilege. With fluctuating hopes and fears as to the result, we determined on one thing, and that was to face all that was involved in the self-activity of children or cease our relations with them.

We were blazing a new path for ourselves and our destination was obscured by uncertainty. Some days we felt confident and sure that we were right. On other days we were assailed by doubts and fears. All the old adages about child training would pop into our minds to intimidate and hold us back. Authority, tradition, and the well-beaten down road which the race had marked out in its journey, claimed consideration from us. Against their claims we had nothing to advance but our faith in life generally, and our belief and confidence particularly in child life.

In the early stages of our resolve for freer conditions our children were allowed to choose the materials they wished to use, but the materials were in the custody of the adults, and the child could only get at the things desired by asking for them.

We had colored wooden beads which were popular with the children. After the children had strung their beads they usually wore them as necklaces. A little girl, named Jennie, was especially attracted to that occupation. Day after day she would ask for the beads. She invariably threaded them in the prismatic order—red, orange, yellow, green, blue, violet.

Jennie had always received a full supply of beads in all the colors, until one day I allowed my fear to overrule me. When Jennie asked for some beads I gave her the usual quantity but only in two colors. Jennie hunted through her beads and then turned to me and said "Why?" I echoed her "Why?" to myself, and answered the little girl by going to the cupboard and getting the rest of the colors for her.

Children had shown us many times that they had a subconscious way of getting at the spirit of a thing. Jennie demonstrated it. She gathered the beads together and put them in her lap. She threaded the beads under the table and kept watching me as if she suspected some interference.

Jennie's attitude revealed to us how sensitively the child records the spirit of an act.

For weeks and months everything had been running along smoothly. We were beginning to congratulate ourselves on the freedom of our intercourse with the children. There was just one thing which we were aware of that we exacted from the children, and that was to answer promptly when the chord was struck on the piano, as a signal for some change in their activity. There was no indication that the children regarded the signal as an interference. The day came, however, when we were aroused from our delusion. The chord was struck for the children to prepare for their work at the tables. The children responded, apparently, but when they had taken their places we discovered that two boys were shuffling along by the wall watching us as if they expected a conflict. The children at the tables were looking from the boys to the adults and from the adults to the boys with anticipation. Inwardly we were very much disturbed, but we assumed an outer calmness that deceived none of them.

We felt hurt by the defiance of the two boys and also at their desire to test our mettle. Years of experience since then has shown us that our chagrin and discomfiture were caused by the old idea, deep-seated in all grown-ups, that the child owed us obedience.

It seemed such a little thing to expect them to do! We tried not to show our disappointment, but the children felt our condition and it created a sense of estrangement in the whole group.

We are able now to acknowledge our indebtedness to the two rebels who braved our displeasure to attain more freedom for themselves.

We can feel but one restriction at a time, yet it is the one and one and one that finally cramps and closes up the life of the individual. The individual who is vigilant enough to combat the one harmless-appearing demand on him, is the one who is fitted to enjoy freedom.

We began the play period each day with the nature plays of the kindergarten, after which the children were allowed free play for about fifteen minutes. One day a little boy, who had my hand in the circle, looked up to me and said, "When are we going to play?" I knew quite well what he meant, but I could not resist the temptation to draw out from him what he thought of the thing we were doing.

"Aren't we playing now?" I asked.

"No," he answered. "These are kindergarten games."

I knew then that the bird, flower and other nature plays were doomed. Reluctantly we relinquished them. They disappeared one by one.

The only room in our building that was large enough for the children to play in was a gymnasium fully equipped for older people. The racks with dumb-bells and swinging clubs were within reach of the children. At first we were fearful that they might be used by them to settle their disputes. We were advised to prohibit their use, but to that we could not consent. Just once we saw a boy grab a dumb-bell and threaten another boy who was going to attack him. The threatened boy discreetly retired, so nothing more happened.

Some adventurous boys learned how to shinny up the swinging rope and land on top of the disk from which a punching bag was suspended. Holding on to the rope they would swing out from the disk into the room. The heavy leather ball at the end of the rope could injure a passing child. We were watchful, but neither warned the child who was swinging nor the children who were below. We wanted to test the value of self-determination in self-development. We were soon rewarded for our non-interference.

We discovered that the boys who had the courage to do the adventurous thing were also the most gentle and considerate. And as they seemed to be able to measure distance, they seemed to be equally able to measure consequences. We have seen boys eager and impatient to take their turn on the rope, standing on the disk with the rope in their hands, shouting down to the children to get out of the way or they would get hurt. Sometimes their call would not be heard below, but not once did we see a boy swing out when he thought there was danger to the other children. This was just one of many incidents which freedom of opportunity demonstrated to us.

We were noted for our noise. Our visitors had to be as healthy in mind and body as our children were, or they could not endure us.

Usually visitors to the kindergartens are sentimental about children. They are most interested in the pretty games and the pretty work under the direction of a skillful kindergartner than they are in any free expression of the children.

Our children were too virile and too independent to be sentimentalized over. We had just one visitor, in all the struggling years, who recognized the meaning and significance of self-determination on the part of the children. We were commonly regarded as iconoclastic and destructive. The visitors shook their heads disapprovingly and predicted disaster and chaos to society if the work were allowed to continue.

I was asked: "What result do you expect from this unrestrained, unrestricted relation to the child?" At that period we were not thinking of results. We were just trying to establish an honest basis with the child. So my answer to that question was, that we did not expect any result during the early years of child life, but we believed that the future life of the child would testify to the truth of our attitude.

Results, however, followed thick and fast, and we soon realized that we were destined to see, in our own lifetime, how life is enriched individually and socially through self-expression. Teachers visiting us could not understand how children without instruction or training could and would do such fine work. Not only were they free from instruction, but we were zealous in keeping ourselves from suggesting or criticizing their work. We believed that recognizing what the child did or could do was all that was needed from us.

The change in the children's attitude toward us was undoubtedly our greatest reward. When we let the bars down and meant that they should stay down; when we determined not to let consequences intimidate us, we found ourselves looking deep into the child's eyes without restraint or barrier. We could laugh back and forth in true comradeship.

The child was getting sure of us day by day, and we were learning to recognize and to respond to him. Instead of sneakingly trying to get his own way, the child would shout to us to look at what he was doing, or invite us to participate in his act.

For a long time after we had abandoned all the grosser forms of restraint or interference, we went through a formal opening in the morning. The children were not obliged to take part in it, but we soon realized that the very fact of introducing such a formality made an atmosphere which was in turn encouraging or discouraging to the children. It was the only esthetic form we had saved from the kindergarten wreck. It was the morning circle—the symbol of unity to us grown-ups. One of our children, however, helped us to cast it aside with all the other kindergarten forms.

One day two little girls offered to prepare the circle for the next morning. As they were arranging the chairs we overheard one of them say, "I don't care about the circle, but mother does; so let us fix it." The girl's words revealed to us that the symbol was becoming an imposition to which the children were conceding as an indulgence to the grown-ups. The abandonment of the circle stripped us of all our armor. Now we were left to face the children each morning in a natural way. I believe it helped us to understand one another better.

In time we concluded that this new situation needed a new name—a name which would convey just what it stood for. So we named it "The Children's Neighborhood Playhouse and Workshop."

And the Playhouse? Just a place where the child could go to express himself and have his neighborhood experience. It may seem like a little thing to you, perhaps, but is it such a little thing? Is it a little thing to have a place for the child to turn to when he leaves his home and thus centralize his outside life so that it may become as real and tangible to him as his home life?

We consider it a great individual and social necessity. We believe that the whole outside world is changed to the child through the actual living experiences which come to him through his neighborhood association. A child who has had early association with his neighbors—it is safe to predict—will go out from his family home to the neighborhood home, to live with his neighbor the life of a comrade.

Incidentally, the child may learn how to do things, in such a neighborhood house; but best and most important of all, is the social experience which free association offers to the child. In free intercourse the child finds himself in an environment where he is free to act and free to get the reaction of his own doing.

Action and re-action are the two great factors in developing self-knowledge in the individual. They supplement and complete each other. An act which is not followed by consequences is void. Expression which is not reflected back to the one who created it, is empty. The re-action must have direct relation to the act—it must be recognized as the outcome of the act—if it is to have any value in the growth of the individual. The act must be a free act and the re-action must be the natural re-action.

Measuring out allowances of freedom to the child is a very unworthy occupation. It places the adult in the position of warden or jailer. Not an enviable relation.

It is difficult for adults to refrain from guiding or directing children with whom they are grouped. Especially so if their center is an educational one. The cause of this, I am inclined to believe, is the lack of personal occupation on the part of the adults. That "Satan finds some mischief still for idle hands to do" is truer of adult life than of child life.

The mischief adults create is not as easily remedied as the mischief of children. Children may disturb or destroy things, but adults cripple and stunt human lives by controlling their energies and directing their lives into channels, which are foreign to child life and out of tune with their real needs.

When I realized how prone I was to intrude myself upon the child socially or otherwise, I resolved to correct it. I took myself in hand and provided myself with work that called my attention away from what the children were doing. I gradually found myself absorbed in my own expression, so much so that I often left it reluctantly when the children called on me to help them out in one way or another. Thus, our relation to the child became more normal and satisfactory when we, too, were spontaneously self-active.

CHAPTER EIGHT

Neighborhood Playhouse and Workshop

When the child reaches his third year—and sometimes before that—he becomes restless and fretful. His conduct indicates a general change in his development. He wants to be taken out and is annoyed when he is brought into the house again. Something in his development urges him to join the life on the outside and at the same time something within him serves to intimidate and hold him back. He does not understand his own need nor does he understand the nature of that neighborhood life which creates in him such conflicting emotions of attraction and repulsion. The child instinctively shrinks from the encounter which he senses he must face as soon as he tries to identify his life with the life of his neighborhood. The child is spiritually attracted and physically repelled.

From the child's birth he has been sheltered and protected by adults. The attention lavished upon him has tended to specialize him as something distinct and apart from other humans. His natural instinct of self-preservation has been intensified by the exclusiveness of his home. He has heard anxious inquiries about the safety of his sled or other toys when they were left out of doors. He observes how the doors and windows are fastened, how cautiously the door is opened when a stranger appears. He has heard his parents discuss and criticize the neighborhood life as if there was no common connection or relation between them. The child absorbs in a large measure the opinions expressed by his parents. So it is not strange to find such children—and they are legion—facing the neighborhood life defensively or aggressively.

Parents recognize that the irritability and restlessness of their child indicate his need for association with other children, but they fail to recognize that the child's need is to associate with the children of his own immediate neighborhood.

When they do yield to the child's demand to be taken out, in nine cases out of ten they dress the child in parade clothes, take him to a park, shopping, visiting, etc. Everywhere and everything but the real need. Tired out from excitement and exhaustion the child returns to his own familiar street, finally sees familiar houses and people, and is then psychologically able to grasp, connect and relate outside peoples and things with his own life, his own inner need.

The day comes, however, when the child is able to formulate his desire, and he then insists on staying in his own street. The insistence of the child forces the parents to yield, and so we find that the long strange journey to a park, etc., is abandoned—for no matter how close the park may be to the child's home, it is far enough removed to give him the impression of strangeness, distance and weariness.

How does the child fare on the street? Usually he is dressed to be a spectator, not a participant, in the street activity. He is sure to be accompanied by a guardian. The guardian may be only an older brother or sister, but he is sure to have the defensive attitude assumed by the home to the outside life, accentuated by the presence of a protector. I have seen children, and so have you, meandering up and down on the sidewalk looking on but taking no part in the street life. The impulse which urged the child to join in the neighborhood activity was a true impulse? and in spite of the child's timidity he would eventually take part in it if he were left free to find out for himself what his desires were. The adult, not understanding the rough and ready play of the street, condemns and disapproves of it. In spite of all the censure, however, the child hears sounds which call to him and he sees things which invite him. The child becomes confused and dissatisfied. He has been taken to the street but he has not shared in its life. Even the boys there have probably not noticed him. If they have, he may have heard a jeering remark about "the sissy." Street boys know at a glance the difference between a free onlooker and a captive and they quickly show their contempt for the latter.

Parents are slow to see that the guardianship which they exercise over the child is a hindrance and restraint to his development. I have never met one who could fully acknowledge it. The child is also unaware that the presence of the adult with him builds a barrier between the children on the street and himself.

I am inclined to believe that plain straightforward domination of the child's life is easier for the child to grasp than the subtle methods which deceive the child into feeling that he has been free while he was being led, influenced and controlled in a way which he could not combat.

Have you ever heard the tone of complaint in a child's voice and seen the look of dissatisfaction in his eyes? How often I have heard that tone and when I have sympathetically turned to look for the cause, I have invariably found a child in charge of an adult, distracted from his real needs, pushing along some expensive toy which only served to irritate the child and further point up his distinctness from other children.

The average child—and that is the child we are most concerned about—must soon succumb to such treatment. The non-realization of the child's desire for free neighborhood association leaves him unsure about himself and also unsure about the life surrounding him. He asked to be taken out from the home and he was taken out. He insisted on staying in his own street and that, too, was acceded to him, and still his need is not realized and his displeasure is more pronounced. The parents are as confused as their child They advise with their friends. Someone suggests a kindergarten or Montessori school.

The friend may recommend one which she knows to be was endeavoring to get away from—appeals to the parents. They investigate, find a group of clean and well-mannered children supervised by charming gentlewomen. They conclude they have found the desirable environment for their child.

The child shrinks from entering the gardens which adults have cultivated for him, but he is unable to put his reluctance into reasonable shape, so his objections—if he advances any—are overruled. The child's chance for free association with other children is completely shut off when he enters the kindergarten. The gentle but firm restraint exercised in the home greets him in his new environment. The child is sweetly taken in charge and appointed to a seat and place which at once circumscribes and limits his power of expression. The child is then pursued by a program which is intended to influence and form his life into a uniform shape which will stamp him for the position he is to occupy in the life of humanity.

The child is more definitely guided throughout the program work than he could have been in the home. The young women are not tormented by doubts as the parents were. They were graduated to accomplish certain results and they set about to do it in a professional and workman-like manner. Every natural impulse of the child they have been trained to regard as indefinite. Their business is to make the indefinite definite.

A perplexed mother related this incident to me. She was searching for desirable association for her child. So she visited kindergarten after kindergarten. In one kindergarten the kindergartner was illustrating a pleasant day in summer on the blackboard. The kindergartner outlined a big square on the board and then turning to the children said, "Now what kind of a sky shall we make for a pleasant day in summer?" No answer. "Can't any child tell me how the sky looks on a pleasant day in summer?" "Jimmie! How does the sky look on a pleasant day in summer?" Jimmie answered, "Gray." "Oh, no! Not a gray sky for a pleasant day in summer. Sara! How does the sky look on a pleasant day in summer?" Sara answered, "Pink." "Oh, no! Not a pink sky for a pleasant day in summer." After much probing for the fixed result one child piped up, "Blue." "Yes, Tommie, a blue sky for a pleasant day in summer." The kindergartner proceeded to fill in a blue sky in her square space.

Tommie, through his chance remark, was favored by a smile from the kindergartner. His answer had relieved her. She was embarrassed for she felt the children were not reflecting credit upon her.

I recall an examination in mental arithmetic when I was at school. We were expected to answer the question without hesitation. Examinations always confused me. I could not think clearly in a competitive contest. When my turn came I gave a random answer. It proved to be correct. Before the examining board arrived, our teacher talked to the class on the approaching examination. She closed her remarks by saying she would smile on the one who reflected credit on the class. She gave me that smile. I felt like a fraud and a cheat. Perhaps Tommie felt the same way over his blue sky. Who knows? I gave no outward sign. Tommie gave no outward sign.

The home kindergarten, Montessori and similar schools divert the child from his own inner need and turn his attention to extraneous things which are foreign to his development. They may introduce abstract things to the child in a Mother Goose fashion, but the jingle does not interpret the abstraction to the child. Even his information is not enlarged by the performance. All these systems and methods only serve to retard the normal development of childhood.

In time the child is ushered into the school proper. The child has had this event held up to him as a red-letter day. The school is endorsed by his parents and all the grown-ups that surround him. Has he not heard the commonplace remark of the adult to the child, "Do you go to school?" "Do you know how to read?" or "When are you going to school?" etc.

In the school, authority and submission are strongly emphasized. In the miniature schools the child was not aware that he was being ruled. The system was more subtle and more effectual because its operation was hidden from the child. He sees that from the autocratic ruling of the school there is no appeal. The relationship is well-defined. All the grown-ups are rulers and all the children are subjects. The child is introduced to the espionage of the monitor and also into an active anti-social society.

The child sees in the classroom human beings without social inter-relationship with them. If a classmate should falter in his recitation the newcomer sees the eager expectancy of the other children to take advantage of their classmate's embarrassment. If the reciter should recover his lost ground, he sees the look of disappointment in the eyes of the majority. If a faltering child should have the answer whispered to him by a friend, he hears the act denounced and the offending child singled out as a disturber.

The ethics of the school gradually initiate the child into seeing his classmates pass through the experience of loss and defeat unaided. The realization also comes to him that there is an outside standard which measures their conduct, knowledge, morals, etc. All must subscribe to the fixed standard or fall by the way into obscurity and disgrace.

The standard is very high. There is only room for one at the top. To gain the top is difficult, for it demands complete surrender of every human natural impulse. When one succeeds he gains the envy of his classmates. When one fails, he falls into the ranks of the envious.

Qualities which have the greatest dehumanizing effect on man and society are the ones which the home, the kindergarten and the school have conspired to develop in the child. It is safe to predict from such training a corresponding development. After the most observant and progressive parts of a child's life have been spent in such surroundings, how can we reasonably expect him to take up his social relations without exercising the faculties which have been aroused, fostered and nourished in him?

Such a human being may be counted upon to take his place in the industrial world as if he were entering an arena to fight for privilege, monopoly, exploitation and defeat of other humans. It is the natural sequence. Why should our young men and women care about their human relationships? They had no opportunity to live in free and equal human association. They have been hindered from realizing their own humanity. They have been treated more like privileged animals than spiritual beings. All the physical attributes have been carefully fostered while the spiritual nature has been ignored and starved.

The recognition which the child needed, when he revolted against the limitations of his home, only an educator could give him. Not a parent, nurse, kindergartner or teacher; far from that. When I claim that he needed an educator, I mean an adult who understands why the child is impelled to leave his home, and why the child must satisfy and realize that need through his neighborhood children; one who is disinterestedly interested in the child as a human being, as a developing social being. And the child must leave his home to find his educator. In a true living center he would have no difficulty, because his need would be anticipated by the adult who realized the child's need, and the necessity to prepare for his coming.

The street conditions are not favorable to true education. The educator cannot be in constant relation with any one child on the street, nor even with a number of children. The street is not adapted for a full and rounded neighborhood association. A great many things happen on the street, but very seldom is the reaction able to follow the act promptly and directly enough to have it recognized as the return of the deed. The strong and forceful child is the only one who is able to express himself and defend his position on the street.

Might is the dominant note in the street. The rights on the street are the ones you dare maintain. Courageous children may protect the helpless ones and defend themselves from the tyranny of the street bully, but that is not enough. It does not ensure a reliable safe center for all children.

The weather conditions also prohibit everyday associations on the street. The most important objection to the street, however, is that the child cannot collect himself nor particularize things readily enough in such a large area. The street life is too general, too vast.

Children reveal the truth of this in their endeavor to limit and define their neighborhood. The boy around the corner is regarded as an enemy. He is fought and driven off as soon as he appears. Gangs are formed in every block, for attack and defense. The child segregates himself and not alone for physical safety but to be able to understand himself in relation to others. It is an effort to narrow his outside relation so that he may comprehend it.

Organized bands express power, intelligence and ability. The young child is too undeveloped to formulate his need so effectively. It is this unfolding stage in a child's development that I am considering and feel most concerned about. The true educator finds in the organized street gang a clue to the child's needs. The educator defines the neighborhood life without hindering it, particularizes it without restraining it, and so interprets to the child his need as a spiritual being. The educator does what the gang does—eliminating the crude expressions of gangdom, i.e., attacks and defense, because they would serve no end in the educational life of the neighborhood.

The educator limits and defines the neighborhood life by establishing a neighborhood house. A house free and common to every phase of life in the neighborhood, be it rough or gentle, old or young.

You may ask why a distinct house? Why not utilize the home of one of the children, or different homes on different days? The spiritual need which urged the child to leave his home, forbids it. Homes are exclusive. For its own preservation the family must exclude the neighborhood experiences. The home is also forced by its very nature to accept the child no matter what his transgressions may be. The child may be reproved for shirking, or imposing, but he cannot be wholly excluded, no matter how his conduct affects the life of the family. He consequently escapes the responsibility of his acts.

The street life shuts out an offender and forces a member of the gang to subscribe to its rules and rigidly obey them. The child forfeits his individual integrity in the gang. In the neighborhood playhouse, the child is in a free environment balanced by consequent responsibilities. Free to act and free to face the aftermath of his act.

A house within sight of the child's home so that he may connect his family house with his neighborhood house, within sight also so that he may realize himself as a free being, going to the Playhouse alone and returning to his home freely and without question; the neighborhood playhouse means to the child opportunity of association with other children on free and equal terms.

Everything in the neighborhood house is shared in by all its members as common property, common responsibility. The very existence of such a house in a neighborhood would make the social life of the neighborhood definite and real to the developing human.

Free access to materials in the neighborhood playhouse would afford the child opportunity to leave his own impression on any chosen material. In this way the child would get the reflection of his own ability or inability, his own power or limitation.

The playhouse should be so constituted that an act may be reflected quickly, simply and directly to its perpetrator; its four walls should serve as an enclosure for personal activity, and at the same time it should sensitively record how the social environment has been helped or hindered, enriched or impoverished by that activity.

Such an educational center revolves around an adult with consciousness fitted to recognize and interpret to the child that the impulses which move the child to action are true and perfectly related to his developing need. The educator must know, as A. E. says, that "the life of the soul is a personal adventure, a quest for the way and the truth and the life."

Parents must understand the mission of the family life and also recognize where its limitations begin, before we can find parents co-operating with the neighborhood activity. The neighborhood life is just as essential to the developing human being as the family life.

Neither the home nor the school is fitted to educate. Education is not the preserving of things nor the learning about things. Education is the development of self-knowledge, self-consciousness through "spontaneous self-activity." Froebel maintained that "man to know himself must make himself objective to himself." Not doing the thing so that others may know, appreciate and value the act, as the home inculcates; not doing the thing to win distinction by excelling others, as the school inculcates, but just doing the thing so that the individual may make his own life concrete and tangible to himself, and thus understand the why and wherefore of his own life.

In true education the observations, experiences and achievements of the child meet with the first consideration. The true educator knows that the stored-up knowledge of the race can only be recognized after man has expressed and revealed himself creatively. The first and greatest need in any human life is to express and reveal his own life. Through his own self-expression the individual realizes that the meaning and purpose of all life is to express itself.

In conclusion I would say that the home is unable to educate. The street area is too vast and lacks the presence of the educator. The program of the kindergarten and the curriculum of the school shut out human everyday experiences; consequently they exclude the opportunity for true education.

Unless the child in freedom verifies what I have claimed as his real need, the neighborhood playhouse idea becomes as much a hothouse product as any other instituted thing planned, carried out and employed on the child by adults.

We believe in it because we have lived in such an environment with the child, and what is more, it was the child who created the environment by gradually eliminating all the symbols and forms of the kindergarten which we sought to preserve because of their esthetic value.

As one child expressed his approval of the playhouse, "Gee! A fellow knows where to find the other fellows!"

CHAPTER NINE

Unity in the Kindergarten

Though the present kindergarten, "pre-school" class and nursery are the outgrowth of Froebel's kindergarten, the teachers seem to be totally ignorant of the fundamental principle of unity in education on which the kindergarten was built. They agree with Froebel that unity is to be achieved in and through individuality and diversity, and yet they insist on uniformity in their relationship with the child.

Froebel held that through *self-expression* man would objectify his desires and impulses and thus develop and become aware of his own nature, his own individuality; and through this consciousness of self, he would eventually comprehend the unity of all endeavor, of all life.

I believe the contradictions which exist in the present kindergarten between what is professed and what is practiced are probably due to the fact that unity as a principle is accepted without recognizing its attributes—individuality and diversity. Confusion arises because unity is dwelt on as oneness. "Unity" is *oneness of spirit*, of life, but not of form. Oneness of form is uniformity, the outgrowth of conformity.

It is generally admitted that all knowledge is the result of discrimination. Discrimination is separation. To isolate one thing from a mass of things gives it distinction, and to that degree individualizes it. When we individualize a thing, we get in touch with the animating principle which characterizes it. In other words, we feel and acknowledge its life when we differentiate a thing from the homogeneous, the universal.

Man can understand life only by particularizing it in a definite, fixed form. He is necessitated by his own power of conception to formulate life so that he may measure and gauge the forms which are indwelling in every form, and which he can comprehend only when he gives identity to the objects about him. This is what man does when he has a sense of his own individuality, and when he recognizes individuality in another.

Everything exists in the universal subjectivity, or subjectively; but man, Froebel declares, is destined to become conscious of his divine origin. It is not enough to *be*, he must know that he *is*. If all of man's knowledge of things primarily depends on sensation derived from contact with the external, then we must conclude that all the consciousness of life that man can ever gain must come to him through the impression made on him through and by means of the senses. While the underlying cause of all manifestation is unity, still no one form can reveal to man the infinite nature of unity. To gain knowledge of life, man must realize it fully in some particular relation. An individual expression, however, while it concretizes and objectifies life, cannot make clear to man the infinite nature of life. Not one form, but variety of form, is essential to reveal life completely; hence the demand for diversity.

When man is able to relate the diversity of individuality to life he has grasped the significance of unity of the spirit. The young child unconsciously manifests the oneness of life, but man becomes aware of this unity through and by means of diversity in individuality; that is, by mentally separating himself from life. Instead of inharmony, the differences in life show him the fullness of life. He sees the diversity of opinion, expression, form, not as an inequality or contradiction of unity, but as a confirmation of it.

A visit to any average kindergarten will convince an educator that Froebel's conception of education is not comprehended as yet. Instead of individuality we find the subjection of the individual; instead of self-activity we find work resulting from either suggestion or direction. Instead of finding the child applying himself to an object that attracts him, going back again and again as long as he finds self-interest in it, as a child in spontaneity and freedom will do, we find a custodian of children, skilled in ways and means to excite, and then, in turn, to quiet the child for some interest of her own which she honestly considers wholesome and helpful for the child. As the professional advocates of the kindergarten say, "The kindergarten tries to *form* the life of the child instead of *reforming* it."

The result of the present method employed in the kindergarten produces an intensity, a precociousness, a superficiality in the child that is not truly representative of childhood at all.

Instead of helping the child to gain true knowledge—knowledge of himself—he is constantly turned away from himself to objects and interests outside of himself. The child is urged to follow a path mapped out by the one in charge of the kindergarten, with no element of his selfhood in it, unless it can be called selfhood when he says, does and moves as he is instructed.

The kindergartner, trained to whip up a flagging interest, keeps the child in constant motion physically, mentally and morally. From the time he enters the kindergarten until he leaves. In such a hothouse the child is forced to yield a return not indicative of his development and natural ability, and so he can gain no insight into his own life.

The child who freely expresses himself and is at liberty to observe the life around him is constantly exercising his full faculties in a natural healthy way. In Emerson's words, "By doing his *own* work, he unfolds himself."

The true educator daily sees many signs in the ordinary life of the child that point to the broadening of his interests and his power to differentiate more and more from the multitude of things around him. The casual onlooker sees nothing of moment in the child's natural development. It is so quiet, so unobtrusive that he fails to grasp its significance.

The young child cannot explain the impulses which urge him to action, nor can he show off attainments which he does not know that he possesses. But there are many tell-tale guides in the daily life of a spontaneous child that will indicate what the child's development is. The things that the child tries to do or succeeds in doing reveal the child's individual capacity or ability.

Adults are often unable to understand the intention of purpose that actuates the child, and conclude there is no consciousness behind his deed. The fact, too, that the form made by the child may be a reproduction of one already existing, tends to lessen its importance to those who do not appreciate the work apart from the intrinsic value of the thing produced, or its originality; and so the child's creation—for a thing is not less a creation because it was expressed before—receives, too often, no recognition. The child must startle and surprise the adult before he can win any sign of approbation. He must leave his normal course and do "stunts" before his action can be recorded as having any merit.

Even in the highest pedagogical circles, this error is very common. A woman who held a position in pedagogy which carried with it much authority said, when her attention was called to some work that was done by a child of six years, "Oh, there is nothing extraordinary in that act; such things are usually done by children of that age."

What an exposure of her real attitude! Was the simple, natural expression relative to the child's own development of no consequence? What worth can an act have for the individual, apart from the normal relation which it bears to the development that formulates it? When we contrast the action of one individual with that of another, we see it out of perspective. We lose its true proportion. Every act must stand alone in its consideration. We fail to understand the real thing, the spirit, the effort and consciousness of the individual, when we separate his act from his own living need and measure it with the act of another.

Every movement of man is in the truest sense wonderful and extraordinary if we refer it back to the development that projects it. The ordinary exists only in the mind that conceives it as such. Walking, talking, etc. are common manifestations of every human being, but they are nonetheless wonderful when a child for the first time demonstrates his ability to walk and talk.

In the present attitude in the kindergarten every effort on the part of the child to individualize himself is frowned upon as an expression of selfishness. Diversity is regarded as disorder. The child's natural effort to establish himself in true relations is repeatedly frustrated by this outside interference. The very number of forty or fifty children in the ordinary kindergarten of today, precludes the child's being able to form any conception of unity with the kindergarten as a whole. No adult or child has the ability to find a living relation with forty or fifty others at once. In large bodies we often find people subscribing to certain conventionalities that hold them as one; but that will not give the individual any consciousness of unity. In such gatherings there is always subjugation of self instead of self-expression.

The first dawn of intellect felt by the individual in thing or person outside of himself will separate that thing or person from the body in which it was previously merged. The separation is caused by his interest in it. To include, man must exclude. The individual must particularize if he is ever to understand the unity of life. He must choose from the homogeneous mass of moving beings someone to whom he can attach himself, and in so doing he must exclude all others until he has related himself to the one whom he has thus differentiated. This law of separation is the basic law of all knowledge and consciousness.

In the kindergarten the attempt of the child to separate himself from the mass or to single out a particular playmate is usually promptly repressed as a sign of weakness in the chain of unity, and the child is wheedled back into the mass from which he had made a feeble effort to withdraw. Not wanting *to do* or *to be* is a negative position, I grant, but we must bear in mind that man gains consciousness as much by rejecting as by accepting.

For example, who has not at some time or other observed little children playing together and overheard remarks such as these: "Come on, Mary, walk with me! Don't play with Susie, I think she's awfully mean." The two then walk off together whispering some secret about poor Susie, whom they leave disconsolate because of the exclusion. Such an attitude is generally interpreted as unkindness, inharmony. Condemning a thing does not explain its true meaning.

To understand her power, the child who extended the invitation to Mary, must do it by testing another force outside of herself. To justify herself, to give herself prominence, she must depreciate Susie in the eyes of Mary, not the way mapped out in ethics, but the natural way mapped out by nature.

The well-intentioned adult sees the act, notes the fact; and without going behind the externality to grasp the motive, the need which prompted the action, proceeds to correct the "evil." The interferer probably succeeds in getting Susie admitted to the group from which she was previously shut out but the experience and realization for which the child was striving is simply side-tracked and postponed.

How long will man foolishly try to change the natural expressions and currents of humanity, instead of trying to understand them? No true knowledge was ever gained by dwelling on the good or evil aspects of a thing; it can be gained only by appreciating the external as an expression of the internal.

In what is considered a well-conducted kindergarten every effort of the child toward self-expression is met with a suggestion by the kindergartner to improve the child's form of expression. This prevents him from receiving any clear impression of his own desire or impulse because the opportunity to objectify it is not allowed him. Instead of making the child's purpose more definite to him—the reason advanced for the interference—he grows more confused, because his own vague purpose becomes entangled with the purpose of another, and so the effort does not return to him the knowledge that his nature instinctively urged him to obtain.

We can assist another to get a certain result, but we can never make the indefinite definite to another. Man makes the indefinite definite *in his own life by seeing and feeling* the reaction of his own act. The more fully and clearly the reaction returns to the individual, the more tangible and complete his knowledge of life will be. Indeed it is the only true knowledge that can come to man.

The greatest menace to the development of self-knowledge in man is an affected, unreal relation, a relation which professes something that it does not fulfill. It saps the integrity of the individual to give him the impression that he is exercising his own free will and choice, when in reality he is performing the will of another, as we find the child in the kindergarten doing.

The child in the public school, while too often addressed in a way that appeals only to a physical sense of gain or fear, holds, after all, a much simpler relation to his teacher than we find with the kindergartner and child.

In the school the relation is not disguised. The teacher insists on getting a certain fixed result from the child, and he understands that he must yield to the demands or suffer punishment of some kind. The child has no confusion about his status. He is well aware that he is a subject under an arbitrary ruler, and that the relation has no element of freedom in it. In the kindergarten, however, the child is led to believe that he is freeborn and that what he does he does from choice, when in truth he is clogged and hampered by subtleties with which he has no power to deal, because he has not the mental ability to cope with them. If a child in the kindergarten "fidgets" under the restraint of imposed activity or inactivity, the kindergartner insinuatingly asks him if he wouldn't like to be a bird or something else that is equally foreign to his own human need. A child's nature is too simple and direct for him to be able to interpret such a proposition to his own uneasy condition. If he is untutored in the ways of the kindergarten, he usually looks abashed when he is so addressed; but a child who is an habitue of the kindergarten knows that such a proposal, at least, will offer a change of occupation, and so he readily assents—unless he is self-poised enough not to be diverted from his own need by any outside suggestion; but that poise is seldom found after the stage of infanthood.

In the school a fidgety child is warned that he will be punished unless he controls himself. Some teachers, it is true, employ the device of the kindergarten, but ordinarily the school attitude is plain and unvarnished, end on that account much healthier for the child. The kindergarten methods confuse and bewilder the child's mental concept of himself and what his need is, while the usual school attitude presses him hard back upon himself and offers him no loophole for escape. The old relation between teacher and pupil may arouse an antagonism in the child, but antagonism is infinitely better for individual growth than the subdued condition which the kindergarten produces.

The child, of course, gains something through following direction. He memorizes and accumulates facts about phenomena and events. The facts abstracted and unconnected to the personal need of the child can give him no grasp of his own life or of any other life. Facts and data are useful when found inscribed on parchment, but in man's relation to man, it is not impression but expression that we feel the need of most. We do not turn to the individual to see how well he can imitate life—unless we want to be amused— but to find in him a personal revelation of life.

Direction and suggestion belong to the province of pedagogy. The distinction between pedagogy and education rests in the difference of attitude. Pedagogy deals with things and the history of things; education deals with life, the spirit, the cause of all form, the purpose of all objectivity.

The form is everything to the pedagogue; the spirit, the purpose, is all to the educator. The pedagogue works for results; the educator works for the sake of the individual, for life.

I see no release for the child from pedagogy as long as the work is left to woman in the kindergarten. Her nature is too preservative, too conservative, to fulfill all the demands of education. Man must again espouse the child's cause before we can in any degree realize the meaning of Froebel. We need the active disintegrating nature of man to rid the kindergarten of the empty formulas which woman has so carefully husbanded as if the forms were life itself.

The shoals that the kindergarten is now in prove that woman is unable to pilot in deep water. I believe the work of education is too great a work for either man or woman alone. Man and woman unitedly must realize the true relation of adulthood and childhood before education can supersede pedagogy. Their very sex differences and tendencies will prove supplementary when they are combined in educating the child. Together they will be strong enough to break up uniformity and see the *unity in individuality and diversity*, which is now so obscured from them because of their present separateness. We must turn to the united man and woman for the emancipation of the kindergarten.

CHAPTER TEN

Discipline

The folly of spending precious time in getting children into positions and postures that there is no good reason for their assuming should be self-evident to any sensible person. On the contrary, the regimentation of young children seems to meet with adult approval.

Grown-ups attend sessions in kindergartens and other child centers and find amusement and satisfaction in the drill which they see young children put through. In fact they visit such places to enjoy the empty formalities to which the children are subjected. The cut-and-dried plan moves along smoothly and that pleases the adult. They are more interested in what is being done with children than in any spontaneous self-active expression of children. The love of forms with adults is almost an idolatry. The centers which they have made for children are, today, practically training camps in which the children are disciplined and prepared for a prescribed machine existence.

I spent a morning in a kindergarten attached to one of New York's foremost institutes. The children—about forty—were seated in a circle, with heels close together and hands folded. The kindergartner was giving an instructive talk on the harvest. A little girl in the circle separated her heels and assumed a less tense posture. The kindergartner stopped her talk and would not continue until the child's heels were glued together again.

The effect of the restraint was soon demonstrated. When the children were permitted to leave the circle, a little girl threw her arms up in the air, gave a yell and ran down the length of the room. She was promptly seized by the kindergartner and locked in an adjoining room. The kindergartner was determined that the yell should not spread. At one of the tables a kindergartner and ten children were seated. The kindergartner told the children she had a pleasant surprise for them. With many devices like, "Now make the fingers kiss," "Now make the little hands hug," "Now let them rest on the table," the kindergartner succeeded in getting the children into a uniform position. The kindergartner then tested the silence by letting a pin drop.

The preparation for the surprise required a great deal of staging. When the form satisfied the kindergartner she affected a great deal of enthusiasm and went for the object. She returned with a large portfolio. The children, worked up to a state of expectancy, unfolded their hands, some leaned forward and a few stood up. With a grieved, hurt expression the kindergartner closed the portfolio, waited silently and reprovingly until every child had resumed his former posture.

A picture was then dramatically uncovered as soon as every sign of interest was gone. It would be interesting to know what conception the children formed of that experience. It seemed stupid to me and wasteful of precious time. To have the young initiated into such artificiality was surely unworthy. All kindergartners are not so obtuse as the one who exhibited the picture. Some are willing and eager to live more freely with the children, but the dread of the visiting committee and of losing their position is too great for them to overcome. The iron hand of discipline is over the kindergartner as well as the school teacher. The kindergartner's work is mapped out for her and she is just as much restricted in her expression as the children.

The program in this kindergarten was on wood. The children showed that they were not at all interested in wood, for they digressed time and again from the subject to their new shoes, clothes, or the new baby, followed up by the kindergartner, who interrupted their confidences by saying, "Now, children, it is my turn."

A little girl seated near the kindergartner looked up admiringly and said, "You have all the turns, don't you?"

Once upon a time children were considered released from the discipline of the school as soon as they had reached the street. Then they could give vent to their pent-up energy by shouting, running, jumping and tumbling over one another. But things have changed! Boys and girls now march two by two into the street, and sometimes continue in that military fashion for a block, the teacher watching them from the doorway and they watching her out of the corners of their eyes, the monitor following and reporting. It may not be too much to expect of the future development of discipline that the children will be escorted by a guard right to their respective homes.

The effect of such drill and espionage is not easily thrown off. It leaves a blight on the young life. I have seen many children, in the sleet and rain, standing in line—soldier-like—waiting silently and patiently to be admitted to the school building. If that military attitude was not exacted from the children it was all the more serious, for it showed the impression the children had received and how it affected their young lives.

Even if such artificial discipline does not succeed in permanently affecting the life of humanity, I am eager for its abolishment because it uses up the time in a child's life that might be used creatively, and also because it encourages the child to evade and deceive.

Petty devices unfit the child for the real experience of life. They shut him off from his childish interests and so retard his natural development.

When we review the arbitrary discipline of the home, school and society, we find an emasculated thing which emphasizes loss and defeat to human life. Every avenue of escape is shut off. A lockstep is instituted in which we may exercise. The trio—home, school and society—have undertaken to develop us so that we may reflect their perfected plan or system. Our lives are to be lived so that we may glorify and exalt them. Their rigid discipline breathes out death. No creative impulse can flourish or grow under its influence. Their discipline is not designed to foster the spirit of life. It is intended to reproduce images of life, to perpetuate old forms of life, and to guard against the creation of new forms.

Nature abhors an imitation, but not so with these self-appointed guardians. They value the imitative uniform thing far more than the genuine natural thing.

The disastrous result of artificial discipline is very evident when we observe how it re-acts upon the child. Listen to his play, "No, you can't have that." "Go right to bed this minute." "Wait 'till father comes home," etc.

The school is represented in the same spirit. The arbitrary authoritative attitude is imitated by the child because it has been his chief and principal experience in his relation with adults. The child represents society by insincere remarks and affected tones of voice. The child simply reflects in his play the impression the home, school and society have made upon him.

In freedom alone can the individual experience the inherent quality which is contained in every existing thing. A quality that never restricts, hinders or coerces the individual. A quality that makes no concession to our weakness, no compromise with our inability.

Equal terms; nothing more, nothing less.

The need of one individual is the need of all, but the manifestation of that need is to be realized in and through individuality and diversity.

As long as a child is kept busy toeing a mark, folding his arms, standing in line, or reciting things in which he has no interest, we shall continue to suffer from uniform expression and mechanical action. As long as we cherish the idea that an imposed task is a good thing for the developing child, we shall continue to divert the child's attention from the real experiences that rightfully belong to a child's life.

CHAPTER ELEVEN

Suggestion and Direction

An unhampered child is always self-active and creative. He is absorbed in his own interests and is therefore reluctant to receive suggestion or direction from the outside. He needs no encouragement to do things. His own impulses and desires are so alive and urgent they keep him busy fulfilling the promptings of his own being. Outside suggestion or direction only serves to interrupt and retard the work of the self-active child.

In the early stages of a child's development he is satisfied with any form which he can create. He is possessed by the spirit of his own activity and finds his satisfaction in the doing of the thing. The concrete forms made by the child reflect back to him his own image and likeness. Through his own activity his vague purposeless feelings assume a shape which make visible and tangible to him the indwelling force which necessitated his activity. He is able to relate the form which he has created to himself because he has not been diverted from his own center by outer forces. He has left his impression on matter and through that impression he has learned the properties of matter. Through his creation he develops a knowledge of himself as a creator. At the same time he recognizes that every visible form exists and is manifested through and by means of the spiritual impulse indwelling in the thing itself. In the degree that he recognizes himself in his acts he is able to understand the case of existing things surrounding him.

In the time and order of a child's development he becomes critical and exacting toward his own work. But before that takes place the form is always subservient to the spirit and we find the child engrossed in his own creations.

When a child is supervised from the outside to do this or that thing, he is not exercising his own power. He may be active, but he is not self-active. He can gain no consciousness of the force in his own nature as long as he is subject to guidance and regulation.

The result of outside direction on the child is a sense of unsureness. Direction implies that the natural inclination and impulse of the child are not in accord with the demand of the outside, so the child is left in doubt of himself and uncertain about his outside relations.

The child who has been subjected to direction is always non-creative, restless, exacting and capricious. He has been trained to look to others for help. If the outside fails to supply his need, he is lost and confused. Guidance becomes such an accepted thing in the life of such a child, that to be left to his own resources for even a few minutes is a cause of complaint. In the midst of his own unexplored nature, his own inexhaustible resources, the child is a beggar—stunted and starved, dependent upon the outside for help because that is where we adults have led him to believe that the source of supply exists.

Who is not familiar with the cry, "What can I do now?" "Give me something to do." "How shall I do it?" "I want someone to play with me," and so on?

When a child is turned away from his own center he is forced to make demands on those who control him. He must be active even though he has no opportunity to be self-active. When the child is spurred on from the outside it is always with the thought of the result. The result is the goal towards which the adult has accustomed the directed child to work. In all relations where suggestion or direction is urged, we are sure to find a standard by which the effort or result is measured and tested. If not in any fixed reward or punishment, then it will be found in favorable or unfavorable criticism, in approval or disapproval. And rightly so, for if the result were not passed upon, the act would be as if it were thrown into space.

I had an experience with a child which showed me the enervating effect of suggestion. A little boy with a slate and pencil was busily drawing the picture of the American flag. He had a small flag spread before him on the table to which he referred for the position of the stars and stripes. He called me to see his work, and when I saw how well he had drawn the flag the idea came to me that if he had material to make an actual flag his confidence in his own power would be much increased. I asked the little fellow to wait for a few minutes and I would give him some colored papers with which he might make a *real* flag—as if the flag he had made were not real.

When I brought him the red, white and blue papers he became excited, and kept nervously asking: "How can I do it? How can I do it?" After some explanation from me, he pushed aside his slate and pencil, eager to take the new thing which promised greater and better results. I had planted the seed of dissatisfaction by suggesting that I would give him something better. For did not my "something-better" offer, imply that his picture was not as good as it might be? The outcome proved that such was the case.

I had no thought or wish for the boy to give a better result than he could naturally produce; but I had made the mistake—common to all interference—in thinking that because he was trying to represent the flag so accurately (for he was counting the stars and stripes) that the colored papers would give him a more concrete and lasting result; for with them I thought he could make an actual flag which he could carry home.

The boy handled the red, white and blue papers. He looked confused and puzzled as if the whole thing were quite separate and distinct from what he had been doing. He finally turned to me asking what he should do with the material. I realized then how I had blundered with the boy, and, trying to repair the break I had caused in his work, I tried to draw out from the little fellow how the colors could be matched and how their form and position might be represented—a thing he was quite aware of before I intervened. He attempted to carry out my suggestion, depending on my help for every move he made, so I decided to leave him alone to recover himself, and perhaps get in touch with the spirit of his own work again. When I returned to him, I found the papers partly cut and scattered on the table. If I had stayed and directed the work he would have had a result, but one not true of his development.

The true return to the little fellow that day would have been the picture on the slate. The picture would have made concrete the child's own need and ability clearly and satisfactorily to himself, while my suggestion only made him feel that the thing he could do I did not recognize, and the thing I could appreciate, he could not do.

> "And all that fruitless individual life
> One can not lend a beam to but they spoil."

Instead of the boy leaving me as one should leave his educator—filled with a sense of his own possibilities and power—the boy left me with his own development and consciousness unrecognized and his effort repudiated. The boy and I both felt a barrier erected between us, and it was my stupid intrusion that caused it. If the boy had been dissatisfied with his own work, he would have had the incentive to try the thing again.

Children are noted for their continued repetition. The same story, the same material, the same game, until they have realized a sense of fulfillment. The sense of non-fulfillment is also a factor in the child's development of consciousness. The child, however, must sense it in direct relation to his own creation. It must not come to him from the outside.

When the child feels satisfied with the form of his creation, it no longer holds for him as vital an interest, but until he senses it as complete he is urged on and on until he perfects it. Concentration, application, and ability can come to the child only through and from his own interest, from his own endeavor. Through his own unfoldment he will absorb, assimilate, and finally understand his own life, and in time the life of humanity.

To be able to recognize his own nature, to become conscious of himself as an entity, the child must have opportunity to exercise his faculties and see himself in the external which he has created. Freedom to act and freedom to receive the reaction of an act is indispensable to self-knowledge.

CHAPTER TWELVE

Value of "Destruction" in Education

Temperamentally I shrink from all forms of destruction. To tear a frock, break a dish or cause a crash is always disconcerting to me. Argument reacts on me in the same way. I deplore this state of being because it has personally caused me unnecessary suffering in my effort to secure for the child an environment in which he might develop freely. I make this "confession of sin" or weakness because it reveals how inclined I am toward quiet and order and how, in spite of my pre-disposition, my experience has convinced me that noise is a healthy factor in the developing stages of a child's growth.

We adults have no way of measuring a child's changing needs. His height doesn't give it. His age doesn't give it. His mental precocity doesn't give it. We can appreciate his need only by the way in which he manifests himself when he feels himself to be free. Consequently, if a big boy expresses himself noisily, it is because he has not developed out of the necessity for noise. When grown-ups express themselves noisily, it is because the noise stage is not outgrown.

When I began my kindergarten studies, the kindergarten system fascinated me with its projects and sequences. The sequences objectified the evolution of one form from another. The process was a symmetrical one which demonstrated order and unity to the last fragment.

All through my kindergarten study, I felt transported. The system enthralled me. Occasionally I saw a child who did not respond to the esthetic process but I gave no serious thought to it. We were taught to use our resources to interest the indifferent child and get him to join harmoniously with the group. When we succeeded we flattered ourselves; when we failed we looked on the child as a problem.

When I became more observant of how children, when they dared, reacted to the imposed orderly forms, I experienced a great shock. It was forced upon me that the child's desire to make a noise or create a wreck was in no way changed by the sequences. The desire lay dormant because the kindergarten preventives left neither time nor place for it; nevertheless it cropped out at the slightest chance and stayed out until it was shooed away by a device.

In my eagerness for an environment without crashes I had quite overlooked the fact that before we were entitled to enjoy such tranquility, it must be the result of an orderly unfoldment from within; that no object lesson with material could convey that truth; that whether we liked it or not we had to wait on development. Furthermore we must see—not endure—in the discordant processes of development, their value, their use and place in the building of a child's consciousness.

As soon as I discarded all methods for capturing the attention of the child I found myself with more leisure to study the child himself, and the things which he created when he was unrestricted. The dynamic child forced one's attention, while the negative child was often overlooked. Separately the children became more real and substantial. Each was endowed with a personality as soon as I ceased manipulating them as a social whole.

I recall my experience with one boy whom I had an opportunity to observe for more than five years. I met Arthur when he first entered kindergarten. He was then three years old. He came each morning with a fresh shirtwaist, bright necktie and hair curled. Arthur was one of three boys and the youngest. Arthur's mother, an ambitious, high-spirited executive woman, had a difficult problem. Her husband, lazy or sick, I never quite knew which, worked rarely, so her income was variable; nevertheless the boys and mother always made a good appearance.

It was my first year of kindergarten responsibility. Our daily attendance was between forty and fifty. In spite of Arthur's attractive clothes and his cleanliness, he did not appeal to me. I happened to look into Arthur's eyes one day and was astonished to find how fiery and rebellious they were. I wondered if the mother insisted too much on the care of his clothes. Arthur's condition troubled me and I speculated on the cause and gave considerable thought to his state.

One day a man interested in education came to the kindergarten as a visitor. Arthur seemed to be attracted to the man and selected him as his partner. The guest would have liked more freedom to get acquainted with the other children but Arthur clung to him jealously. When they were seated beside one another, Arthur suddenly turned and looked into the man's face and asked, "Will you tell my mother if I swear?" The visitor was so astonished that he gave no answer. I suppose Arthur felt that he was safe for, the guest told us later, Arthur put his head on the man's knee and poured out a volley of oaths. The process was very painful to the visitor for he wondered where the child acquired such language and why he needed to express himself in such a manner. Arthur, however, seemed more relaxed and calm after the violent outbreak. No reference was made to the act so Arthur had no fear of reaction from it.

When Arthur reached his fifth year his mother became janitor of the Guild House, in which the kindergarten was held. Janitors represent great power to children. They are much higher in the power scale than teachers. I have often heard children discuss the authority of janitors. Arthur seemed to be imbued with the same idea for he assumed a very superior air and I frequently saw him bullying and bossing other children. When Arthur saw that I was aware of it, he would turn right around and pretend to be doing the child a service. Ordinarily I would have reflected the impression such conduct made on me, for I was then and still am a strong believer in the value of reaction. Instinctively, however, I felt that Arthur's case called for release more than reaction. The inner spring of his life seemed to be poisoned.

When Arthur discovered that his road was clear so far as the kindergarten was concerned he developed an objectionable "ward boss" attitude. He was more alert mentally than the other boys of his age. He was full of plans and knew how to execute them. He felt his power and he rejoiced in flaunting it. He became the accepted leader of a circle of boys who paid tribute to him by endeavoring to carry out his commands. Arthur exulted in his position and played with the group as if they were so many pawns on a board. When he felt quite sure of his group he hungered for wider conquests, so he began, with his gang, to experiment with his environment as a whole.

He planned a structure built up entirely of the second Gift blocks. He induced his group to select the second Gift and to use them in the construction. Arthur aimed to have a high building, which required skill to erect. The slightest deviation might cause the building to topple. Arthur was very exacting about the task and often excluded a boy who seemed incapable of the careful standard of work. When the building was completed, Arthur revealed what was in his mind. He or a favored boy would fire a wooden ball, part of the second Gift, at the building which would fall with a great thud. Every child in the kindergarten seemed to enjoy the crash. I was the only one who suffered. Arthur, in due time, became aware of my recoil from the crash. Sometimes I would leave the room when I expected it to take place but Arthur would wait for my return and impishly enjoy my discomfiture. Arthur must have psychically gotten hold of my state because outwardly I gave no sign and never referred to it in words. Arthur would go into ecstasy and jump and laugh over the fact that I had not escaped. When I saw that he seemed to enjoy his power to make others suffer, I concluded that I would stand my ground and let Arthur drink a full cup of satisfaction. Day in and day out the structure went up and the crash followed. I resigned myself to the martyrdom for I believed if

Arthur's feelings were again imprisoned, his whole manhood would be wrecked.

One day the structure went up; there was a long wait. One boy impatiently asked, "When are you going to throw it down?"

"We're not going to throw it down, we're going to take it down" was Arthur's answer.

The blocks were taken down one by one and that finished that experience. We never returned to the crash. It was not suppressed, it was *outlived*.

One time when Arthur returned to his work table he found another boy there interfering with his work. He began to treat the boy roughly. I knew what was going on but I avoided looking in that direction. Suddenly Arthur stopped and made believe that he was just skylarking. I looked about for the cause to see his mother standing in the doorway with flushed face and angry eyes.

I went over to her and said, "I wondered what was the matter. Don't disturb the boy."

"You didn't see what he was doing," she answered. "He was beating the other boy."

"Oh, yes, I know quite well what he was doing. The boy wouldn't give Arthur his place so he forced him away."

That led to a serious talk with Arthur's mother later. I asked her to let Arthur stay in the kindergarten until I felt that he was ready to leave. She responded to my appeal and Arthur stayed until he was eight years old. He then went to the Public School next door and was graduated from the grammar school at twelve. When he first went to the school, Arthur's father came to me and said that he didn't know that I had been teaching the boy reading and writing. I said I had not, but Arthur was bright and had picked it up immediately. Perhaps it is too much to hope that Arthur got rid of all his mean kinks during our five years together, but enough was released for his spirit to flow more evenly. I saw him when he was graduated from grammar school and he seemed a normally poised boy.

I feel quite sure that if Arthur's infant environment had not been so hedged in by taboos, he would have worked off the desire for noise and crash in his infancy. A boy with his executive ability would then have realized more through his power to build than his power to destroy.

Banging a spoon on the table; throwing things from the table to the floor, are activities of delight to the infant. The infant thrives on the clatter he causes. These are important outlets for infant energy and equally important inlets to his consciousness. He creates the noise so he feels it is a part of himself. When these avenues of expression are closed to the infant by no, no! or slapping of the hands, then we may rest assured that it cannot be skipped. That stage of development must be outgrown. It can be outgrown only by outliving it.

Many years later I came in contact with a boy who had been restrained by loving methods. He had an invalid mother, a highly nervous father and was in the general care of a governess. He had no street experience. Once a day he was taken to the park or museum. John came to us when he was about five years old. He seemed to be quite self-centered and self-employed. One morning John came to the play room quite early. There were no other children present. In a short time I heard a loud noise. When I investigated I found John with a croquet ball which he banged from one end of the large room to the other. Every time the ball struck the baseboard it left a dent. I was concerned about the damage, for the house was relatively new; but the boy's fury indicated that he was hammering away at all the things which had held him in his infancy and which now restricted him. This was his opportunity to take his revenge. I kept out of the room. I was the only other person in the house. I made no comment. John dared to do many things later that we never dreamed he would be interested in. One day his father saw him engaged in a fist fight with a boy from a neighborhood tenement house, and John was packed off to a boarding school. John is now busily writing rebellious plays that remind me of the croquet ball.

The value of the desire to destroy, to tear down, (the crash, the noise) in the developing life of the individual is commonly overlooked, when it is not condemned. Froebel said education is twofold: active and passive. Most educators seem to interpret educational activity as a series of preventives. When a child builds with his blocks and then exultingly smashes it down, the educator gently shows him a better way. Sometimes the child complies for the suggestion diverts him from what he was doing, but let us not deceive ourselves into thinking that the device in any respect fills the place or need of the crash.

The crash is one thing; the orderly taking down of a structure is another; it represents an entirely different state of consciousness. One cannot be substituted for the other. The crash conveys to the crude consciousness a sense of power. The crash delights him because it is direct and convincing. In the crash the child recognizes his control over the material and also over his environment. The child is necessitated by the law of development to gain all consciousness through the external reaction. He must have freedom to externalize his desires and feelings so that he may concretize and make visible to himself the forces which move him to action. When the young child constructs, it is an outer manifestation of a subconscious state. It reveals acquired and developed power. When, however, he attacks and tears down his own construction or the construction of others, it is because he is objectively after new experience, new knowledge. It is the child's form of analysis.

I am not considering the acts of rebellious or perverse children. I am considering the necessity which actuates the average child and his normal endeavor to get some grasp on his own life in his own way. When the natural outlet or inlet is closed against the child's direct physical manifestation of power, there and then the mischief begins. He employs his mentality to plot and plan how to accomplish the hindered activity and thus the process of development is prolonged.

The child must realize himself first in the physical. If we insist on repudiating that step in his growth and try to promote him into the mental and spiritual plane, we distort and maim his life. There is no fixed line between physical, mental and spiritual development. They are inseparably one and the same.

CHAPTER THIRTEEN

Play

Through play the child makes an inquiry into the life surrounding him. He tests the force which he feels in himself and which he sees shown by others. The form of the child's play is the outcome of his sense impressions and observations. He endeavors to identify himself with his environment by imitating, impersonating the life about him. In his play he is in his laboratory, analyzing and synthesizing the things with which he is familiar.

Two events in my own childhood mark very forcibly the different forces at work when a child plays.

My grandmother had a muff which seemed to me a very wonderful affair. Its size, its quality attracted me greatly. Finally I made up my mind that I must secure the muff and go out from my neighborhood with it. I stealthily removed the muff from the box, held it by its tassel behind my back, and walked backward until I was on the street and safely away from the house. Where should I go? I recall that to walk on the street with it was not enough. I wanted to give the impression to someone that the muff was mine. I thought of a family that lived about a quarter of a mile away from my house. It seemed many miles to me, but that only served to enhance the adventure. When I reached the house, no one was at home, so I seated myself on: a "settle" in the kitchen, my hands in the muff, and waited. A young woman of the neighborhood came in, saw the funny side of the situation, began to laugh and said, "Hello, Sissy, where did you get the muff?" Instantly, my whole play was shattered. How I hated her and her haunting laugh.

After she went out, I got down from the "settle," grasped the muff by its tassel, put it behind me and trailed it back home. I entered my home unobserved and put the muff in its box. I did not get over my hatred of that woman until I had outgrown the event.

In the city where I was reared, the French-Canadians used to do tailoring work for clothing concerns. I was very much interested in their coming and going. The way in which they carried their work made a deep impression on me. It was always neatly folded and carried hanging over the left arm. One day I made up my mind that I would impersonate one of these tailoresses. I went into a doorway, took off my jacket, folded it neatly and let it hang over my left arm. Then I walked down the street where the clothing houses were. At the first one I came to I walked up the steps, took off my jacket, as if I were delivering work, refolded the jacket, replaced it on my arm, and walked down the steps to the street feeling quite satisfied that every passerby would take me for a tailoress.

An infant may see many things about him but out of them all he may distinguish only a piece of paper. If he is able to get the paper, he will just as surely begin to tear it. The earnestness of the infant, the satisfaction which he feels, is shown in the expression of his face and his absorption in his act. When the infant has satisfied his need, when he has realized from the experience all that his play with that object held for him, he masses the parts together with a slap as if his intention were to restore the fragments into a whole again. The infant then abandons that occupation and endeavors to grasp another thing within his observation. A child's plaything is no longer of any value to him when he has gotten from it what he was striving after. Through the external form the child works his way inward to the internal cause. The child is attracted to the things which correspond to his developing need. He responds to the forms which his state of consciousness can comprehend; his response reveals that in some degree he feels their relation to his own need. This is verified by the child's actions. If this recognition or feeling were not subject to the law of his own development, the first thing seen or presented would influence him to seize the object or imitate the act. The child does not observe or represent everything which occurs about him. He simply draws in from the outside what he requires and can use.

The child is not more subject to conditions surrounding him than is the common plant. The plant is not subject to every ingredient common to the soil in which it is rooted. It chooses and draws in the elements needed for its nourishment and growth; just the things which it can use and assimilate to enable it to evolve its own particular form of life according to the law of its own inherent nature. If it were otherwise the external would cease to be a revelation of an internal force. Form would no longer reveal an indwelling life. Form would be merely an accumulation or aggregation of matter.

The child, like every other manifestation of life, saves himself. His state of consciousness shields and protects him from the intrusion of things which have no relation to his developing need. The child is not so entirely at the mercy of grown-ups as we believe him to be. Grown-ups are more often deceived by the child than they are aware. Some adults feel their impotency in dealing with the young, but they are loath to admit it and prefer to keep up a semblance of influence. The child is forced, in the strained relation, to adopt a camouflage for the adult, and the adult in turn tries the same game with the child.

Must this prevalent insincerity continue? Is there no way out? Of course there is. Discard all the sham superiority and artificiality which are now employed; give the young a chance to express themselves creatively; fill your own mind with the truth that the law of human development must restore order out of the present chaos and confusion which our own stupidity has created. When our whole being is filled with the belief that life cannot repudiate itself, we shall radiate it outwardly and thereby fill the young with trust and confidence.

Play is the clearest reaction of the spirit of man. When infant, child, youth or man plays, the floodgates are opened, the spirit of man is released. In his imagination man transcends the limitations of mind and body. He is transported above fear or constraint when he plays. Embarrassment, ridicule and criticism are shafts which cannot reach him so long as he dwells in the spirit and continues to manifest his spirit in his daily living. When the spirit of the adult is free—even relatively so—he plays. Whether the form of his play be grave or joyful, matters little.

There is no clear line of demarcation between the infant and the child, between the child and the youth, between the youth and man; one stage merges into another gradually and harmoniously when no impediment or obstruction is put in the way of the young.

When, however, the child's play is guarded or directed he has no freedom of opportunity, no chance for selection or self-expression. He cannot draw out from the mass of things surrounding him the particular object which he has observed and needs to test before he can understand it. When his play is directed, he plays not at all. He is simply a puppet in the hands of another. When the adult has to enforce the rule of a game, it proves that the game is one of the adult's choosing and that it either does not interest the child or that he does not understand the necessity for the rule. When children play freely and naturally they demonstrate over such superficialities. They are exacting to the last degree, often putting a child out of the game or breaking the game up if the rule of the game is not observed.

When we understand the true meaning of play, we shall prize it as the simplest form of revelation in human life. We shall then know that to be able to see and study the spontaneous, self-active child, will be the greatest privilege that can be granted to us, and we shall watch jealously for every opportunity to see the *self* expressed, because it will be to us a means to the understanding, not only of child life, but of all human life. This consciousness can come only to him who has developed a genuine appreciation of the innermost meaning of life, who has a vital grasp on his own life.

In every department of science, only the greatest scientists are capable of passivity; only they have anything to sustain them in their long watching and waiting, only they are able to appreciate the significance of commonplace expressions.

It is said of Darwin that he watched and studied frogs for twenty years. When shall we be able to tell of having studied children for so long, not in the study room or on paper, but in the open of the child's own life? And studied without any ulterior motive, without self-interest, except the one great interest that should ever unite adulthood and childhood—the unity of life.

The test for earnest seekers after truth—no matter what field—is, keep your hands off! Wait and observe the life in its freedom, and the truth will be revealed to you.

But it may be said that the need of opportunity for the child to play has had the public ear for many years. Large sums of public money have been appropriated to further such opportunity. Organizations have been formed to direct play centers. Every park has its allotment for play. Piers and playgrounds are equipped as play centers. And yet we find the child undernourished, anemic and undeveloped spiritually, because he is not expanding in his natural element, which is play.

After studying the playgrounds for a period of three years, I concluded that the playgrounds and similar places are merely outdoor gymnasiums. They are fitted up to answer the needs of adolescent youth and adulthood. They are too remote from one another to be living neighborhood centers.

The human elements that congregate in such centers are alien to one another; they are there as separate entities. The playgrounds are planned and equipped as special places to be used at special times, like baseball or football fields. Frequently they are used as mere loafing places for youths of both sexes. Marauding gangs looking for adventure in the form of exploitation, monopoly or just plain fight, are often in evidence.

Young children cannot go to the playgrounds unaccompanied, not because the playground rules them out, but because they would have no chance to use any of the things furnished there. When children are accompanied by caretakers they are usually initiated into an anti-social life; they are, even when just infants, put into swings and kept there after they have fallen asleep. To get and hold privileges seem to be the common endeavor. Instead of socializing the human, such places seem to call out anti-social traits.

Society has conspired to utilize the child's energy as we have learned to harness steam, electricity, gas, etc. We have observed that the ceaseless activity of the child has some constructive value, so we try to control and guide it in order that it may return a dividend to society.

The reactionary effect of the public play centers has been caused by the attitude of society toward the young. Adults have tried to protect themselves from annoyance and destruction of property by attempting to segregate the young in set places. They have counted without their host.

The real value of a child's natural expression is entirely overlooked when we strive to control, direct, suggest or in any way change the course of the child's play.

But what have I to offer in place of all the things that I would abolish? Well, I too would establish play centers, but in every neighborhood. Mine would include the whole block, for I would go back of the city houses, tear down the fences and utilize the wood for a playhouse which I would build in the center. If the wood were not fit for building purposes, I would pile it in the center and make one great bonfire to celebrate the event. With the barriers removed, the work-a-day life of the neighborhood would be seen.

The social life would be extended, for the "gang" from around the corner would no longer be an enemy, but would be an integral part of the community life. The equipment would be erected by the members of the community as they felt a need for it. The leader or director would be selected because of his natural qualifications. The adult or youth with the sincerest play spirit would naturally form the center of such a group. Indeed there might be many centers because there would be many groups with varying needs in such a community.

Children have always rebelled against back yards. The barriers reacted unpleasantly on them so they chose to play on the street because it was more open by contrast. With the fences abolished, there would be no back yards. The child's world would be enlarged. Instead of taking a journey in order to find space in which to play, the child, adolescent youth and adult would open their back doors and step out into their real social life which would be that of their own immediate neighborhood. The back of the house would then be seen as the real, genuine, vital part of their separate homes. All the necessary functions of home-making are performed in the rear of the house. All the sham and make-believe are displayed in front. The over-dressing of children for street parade, the temptation of ice cream cones, lolly-pops, chewing gum, etc. would be removed, for every home in the block would serve to remove the thing extraneous to its need.

The dissipation of the movies would also be overcome, because from the larger human contribution there would be distraction and entertainment sufficient to make them forgetful of the unrelated outside life. Not much money required to erect such structures—just removal of the existing barriers.

"Simple! Why, that's the old woe of the world."

Nevertheless we must return to simple things or we shall have a great reckoning one of these days.

Even the families as a group would form a healthy, social life. Fathers and mothers would soon rekindle the spark of play, which is smouldering in every human, as soon as opportunity was offered and restraint was removed. When the child sees the parent play, his own instinct and impulse to play become real and tangible to him. When the adult reveals to the child that he too has the impulse to play and that he obeys that impulse, the child gets from such an adult a verification of a continuity in life. The child's imperative need to play assumes a dignity that serves to connect, enlarge and enrich his life. First the child feels and later understands that play is a continuous, permanent expression of all forms of life; that the law of development demands that every living thing must express and reveal itself in play.

Once the play spirit is aroused in man, it should stay with him through his whole earth experience.

Age does not herald in play. Play is not excluded or prohibited from any period or stage of life.

CHAPTER FOURTEEN

Why Does the Child Play?

There is no period, I believe, in the child's life or stage of development that the adult understands so little as the playtime of childhood.

Perhaps never in the history of man have we heard more concerning the importance of that period than at the present time, but behind it all we find that the child's play is not the real consideration, but how the adult can utilize the self-activity of the child to perpetuate or advance some idea of his own.

We so familiarize ourselves with fine phrases, without analyzing them or even attaching much significance to them, that we find no contradiction when we talk of "development through spontaneity and self-activity," "learning through play," etc., and in our actual relation with the child we attempt to teach through and by means of the child's play. Instead of allowing the child to receive his own impressions from the result of his own activity, we constantly try to leave our impression upon him by governing every attempt to express himself self-actively.

We hear, too, of "freedom restricted," "freedom under the law." The first word precludes the last and the last contradicts the first. No one can give freedom to another; each one must earn it for himself. When a man is free he is without limitation. He cannot be under the law because he then *is the law*. Rule or privilege is what such advocates have in mind, not freedom. Man juggles with words as he does with things, neither comprehending nor realizing that they have any real meaning of their own.

The adult, finding himself in daily contact with children who express their needs in simple ways, takes it for granted that he knows all about them. Because a child's hand is so soon filled, as the German proverb says, every well-meaning but ignorant adult thinks he knows how to fill it. Everything seems easy to the individual when his knowledge of the thing is limited.

The adult can be fitted to appreciate and live with the child as an educator only when he has realized that through his own experiences a consciousness of the depth and capacity of life, no matter what its form, can be gained.

If it is acknowledged that the circumference of the pea has as many degrees as the circumference of the globe on which we live, then it is not claiming too much to say that life is the same in its degree and relative capacity whether embodied as a child or adult.

The child's life is just as complex in its nature as the life of the adult. His experiences, according to his need and ability, are just as vital and hold as much for him as any experience of adulthood can hold for adult life.

Life is so modifiable, looking out upon it; abstract principles are so easily adjusted, in the abstract. On paper it is simple to deal with a child. In the ordinary household, kindergarten or school he is looked upon as artificially as if he were on paper, only he is worse off because the harmless theory is inflicted on the child in those relationships.

Divorced from the natural, free life through which he could find himself, the child becomes in these restrictive relationships plastic and pliable. This leads the majority of adults to conclude that it is the child's nature to be so. Books are written on the subject, statistics are taken (stutterings according to Dickens) on the pliability of the child and how to utilize it advantageously in education.

The truth is that *self-preservation* forces the child to *assume* those characteristics. He follows the law of the least resistance. The child allows the adult to have his own way for the time being and merely waits for his own opportunity. If the child does not thus adapt himself to the conditions imposed upon him, he would be destroyed in such an unequal contest.

Self-preservation is found in nature strongest in the lowest forms of life. The same holds true of *states of consciousness*. The more undifferentiated the form or state, the greater the power of preservation. Cunning, strategy, deceit and lies are the means in a restricted relationship whereby the child eludes the adult, attains his own end and saves himself.

The child simply obeys a natural law in this. All nature shows it. When a stream flows along freely and meets an obstacle, it travels under and around it, thus gaining its destination with the *greatest economy of force*.

As little of the true nature of the child is known when his activity is restricted or directed as we can learn of the natural characteristics of animals in menageries. Every effort of the animal in confinement is bent toward attaining its liberty, or in hopeless dejection it crouches sullenly in a corner of its cage—perhaps never in its whole imprisoned life showing a natural trait.

The restlessness of the confined animal gives the impression that its only object and purpose in life is to attack and devour—which is not true of it under natural conditions. It attacks and devours when free, not for the sake of destroying but to satisfy hunger. John Muir claims that bears prefer strawberries to human flesh. The facts derived from observing a controlled form of life are not worth the time so spent because they are not true of the natural life at all.

The small part that the animal plays when his trainer is demonstrating his ability to control the animal in the cage or circus is a good illustration of the attitude existing between adulthood and childhood generally. People do not visit the circus to see what the animals can do, but to see how the trainers have succeeded in subjecting the animals. When the kindergarten or school is visited it is for the same purpose, to see how skillfully the teacher in charge manages and influences the actions of the children.

The searcher after truth never devotes himself to the quackery of improving life, but seeks to understand life as it is—not as he would like to shape it.

105

Every manipulation in nature demonstrates the futility of any control in establishing any permanency. It is well known that as long as control is exercised man gets partly or in whole the result aimed after. But let the restriction be abandoned, and the suppressed force begins to spring forth as if no influence had ever been brought to bear on it.

Under cultivation pigeons exist in a great variety of forms, but when left to themselves they revert to their primitive form. The gardener succeeds in shaping the force in the pansy until it has yielded its fullest color and size, but by the end of the season it tends to return to its original state, the little "Johnny Jump-up." This seems to be true of every directed force in nature.

If the forms of life in the lower kingdoms cannot be affected permanently by direction, how can man rationally hope to change the life of humanity where the force is so intensified on account of the additional powers of expression?

The ordinary conception of a child's play is that it is a form of amusement or a time of abandonment to the fanciful, the unreal. That is a purely superficial view.

I have observed children closely for many years, and the result has convinced me that play to a child is what religion is to the adult. It is an earnest and serious inquiry into the nature of life through and by means of an external form.

The child's play is the result of observations which he analyzes and then synthesizes. For example: the child is surrounded by many objects. He sees many things but he observes out of them all, possibly, a piece of paper; he secures it and proceeds to tear it. The earnestness of the child so engaged testifies to the truth of the claim of psychologists that this form of destruction is a searching after a cause. The child frequently tries to mix the parts into one another again and thus synthesizes what he had previously analyzed. Children do the same with their blocks. They discriminate by choosing parts of the whole, constructing with them, and then crashing them down. The child not only senses his power in his ability to demolish form, but the act merges the analyzed and synthesized parts into the universal again, from which they were evolved. The casual onlooker simply sees a change of mood without purpose behind it. The child's investigation completed, the thing has no more value for him. He does not care for *things*, but he is searching after the *cause* of things—not with a personal consciousness, but the law of development works just as surely and truly whether man has any consciousness of the law or not.

The child rarely laughs at his play (I mean when he plays, not when he is played with by the adult), there is too much involved in it. When the adult plays with the child, he either takes up the form of play peculiar to children or else he plays down to them. Children, I have noticed, seem a little puzzled and perplexed at the antics of the adult. The relation then passes into that of amuser and amused. The child takes up the excitement and it becomes a frolic; indeed it is no longer play to the child but diversion.

The child, when he plays, strives by means of imitation or representation to identify himself with the characters he impersonates. To identify himself with the lives of others, he must assume the form of life observed and analyze it. It shows the child's endeavor to grasp the meaning of the unity, the oneness underlying the universal. He merges himself in it, assimilates it, and thus makes it a part of his own life by doing the thing he saw done.

A little grandniece of mine would pretend to be different characters that she had heard about or met and then would insist on my calling her by the name that she was impersonating.

Play, to be play, must be a spontaneous, free expression of the child. When we find adults busy correcting or substituting other forms of play for those employed by the child, we can see clearly that the child's need is not understood and the importance of play to the child is not comprehended at all.

The child sees many things passing before him, but he observes only those things that rightfully belong to him, i.e., the things that he can respond to. The response evidences that he recognizes them as having some relation to himself. If the recognition were not the result of the law of his development, the first thing seen or represented in the external would affect and influence him, and a desire to seize it would possess him, and so on in the order of things. This we know is not true if we have studied the child's life at all, or if we have any remembrance of our own lives. The child does not observe and imitate everything that occurs about him. He draws in from the outside what he needs.

CHAPTER FIFTEEN

Rough and Tumble Play

When the noisy "rough and tumble" play of children is neither valued nor appreciated by grown-ups, we usually find them trying to counteract the child's rough play by introducing forms that they trust will develop qualities and virtues which may change its conduct, and thus prepare a basis for a higher state of individual and social development. They look upon the child's "puppy dog" play as an animalistic survival which should be supplanted by games which emphasize a more advanced stage of growth. Therefore, even if the child is not forbidden to "roughhouse" he is cajoled or diverted from it. When boys, just for fun, spring at each other and hit the floor with a bang, adults, particularly women, feel that it is barbaric. When an older child teases a younger one or tries to provoke a younger to fight, the older child is usually admonished for taking unfair and mean advantage over the younger. I also suffered from such delusions and preached many an unheeded sermon to the children when complaint was brought to me or I happened to witness such acts. I learned, in time, that every child went through the same process. The children who wept and complained yesterday, were practicing today the same tricks that they had grumbled about.

Finally I asked myself, "Whom should the child tease when he is itching for physical contact or conflict? His equal or superior?" Self-preservation forbids that. He is just experimenting with adventure. Later on he will disdain such unequal combat. We have no power to change his impulse. Neither coercion nor coaxing is effective. There is nothing left to us, but understanding of, or retirement from the child's world.

Through the necessities of his own, life the child creates a world of his own. A natural barrier is erected between all grown-ups and children by the normal needs of child development and the normal needs of adult development. Antagonism arises because adults try to graft their needs onto the needs of child life.

It is very difficult for the adult to admit that there is a place in the child's world from which he should be excluded; not excluded arbitrarily, but because his body is too old and he has lost his taste for or outgrown their sport. When the adult realizes that it is his own physical, mental and spiritual attitude that shuts him out he will cease to invade the child's world, and may then find that he has a very important link with the young. The young will demonstrate it by approaching him when they feel the need and that need will crop up much oftener than one is likely to think.

When pussy cats crouch, spring, use claws and teeth an one another; when dogs chase, attack and again pursue one another, there seems to be some comprehension that through such play the animals are fitting themselves for the struggle to exist. Why not include the natural activities of children as a preparation for future living? When we grasp the relation between a child's impulse to "rough it" and his developing need as a human being, we shall find that we have bridged the chasm which now separates the young from the old.

Artificial conditions help to breed artificial states of being. Hothouse treatment tends to foster a general exotic state favorable to delicacy, cowardice, morbidity, sex curiosity and sex precocity. When the child does not feel the urge to swim, climb, run or fight, he cannot experience the healthy relaxation that comes from being "good and tired." The spiritual urge that energizes the physical body of the active child, exhilarates and transports him beyond physical pain. Fear, suffering, consequences have no potency as long as the spirit dominates him.

Even though I shrink from violent combat I have been forced to admire the heightened color, flashing eyes and taut nerves of combatants. Contrast such children with those who have yielded to the inducements and protection of the old and you will find pallid, limp, shrinking creatures who have been deprived of their birthright. They retire to corners where they pretend to be interested in books. Their playmates, however, are not deceived by the "bluff" and they soon become the butt and jest of the active ones. They gradually shrink more and more away from the active life around them and in time they become victims of their own sensuous natures.

When the senses (the physical feelings) gain the ascendancy children are tossed about like puppets. Every scratch is turned into a wound. A splinter starts the tear flowing, cold paralyzes them, heat exhausts them. The senses, instead of serving them, become their master. Their lives are soon converted into indulgent orgies. Neuroticism appears in all their actions. The physical body, having no healthy activity to expand and contract, insists on being heard. It is like a spoiled child that is left unoccupied and so becomes restless and peevish. In time such children are initiated into sex practices. Starved spiritually they gorge themselves physically, and so we have our psychopathic problems created by our own stupidity.

I have been in kindergartens where such a fetish was made of quiet, rest, order and estheticism that the subtle pressure became unbearable to the children. A few, when they dared, showed a wicked resentment and would go out of their way to hurt someone or to injure something in that environment. I recall one morning when we were all seated in a circle with a potted plant in the center—it was the story period—a boy rushed from his seat to the middle of the ring and kicked the potted plant. He was quickly taken in hand and prevented from any further exhibition of protest.

Less forceful children, suffering from ennui, took refuge in sex indulgences. In spite of the kindergartner's vigilance to keep the children's hands engaged in some form of work, such children could not be controlled. Frequently a child would be sent home with a note asking the mother to keep the child away until the tendency was overcome "because such a child is a bad example to other children."

If the young woman were not so far removed from the basic requirements of the children, when she discovered such practices she would have sensibly shoved back every chair and table in the room and turned the children loose with one another. The rebels would then find opportunity for activity and the quiet, self-indulgent ones would have no chance for unhealthy indulgence in a bustling, noisy group of spirited children. Father Loyola said, "Where there is much noise, there is very little sin."

The noisy plays of children reveal their eagerness and sincerity. The whole world may see and hear them. They have nothing to conceal. On the other hand, when they are doing things with a sense of guilt, they are quiet enough, because they do not want to attract attention.

The hearty play of children should sound like triumphant music to those intimately associated with children. A grown-up can gauge pretty well what is happening in a group of children as long as they can be heard. Adults may be concerned about furniture, etc. when boisterous play is going on. The solution to that is to have plain and substantial things in their environment. Things fit for wear and tear. If children's normal noise is disturbing to adults they should remove themselves and go into retirement until their own neurotic condition is changed into normality.

We have had too much fitting in of children to the condition of tired fathers, mothers, sleeping babies and, to cap the climax, teachers. It is therefore not surprising that there are such records of vice among children and youth. It is like a reaction against the shutting down of their natural energy. If adults have weighted down the safety valve of childhood, they must face the consequences.

When you analyze noise you find that it is an aggregation of sound in a confined space. The same sounds in the open cease to be noise. Children are not disturbed by noise. I have often observed adults cover their ears and have a nervous tremor at some sudden bang when children were not bothered at all and would not even look in the direction of the sound. I never saw children show any nervousness or physical distress because of noise. They are more likely to join in and help increase the volume of sounds as if they enjoyed it.

When adults are more normal in their attitude, there will not be so much abnormality in children. When we recognize that rough and tumble play is as useful to the child's growth as it is to the animals, we clear the ground of many noxious weeds.

I know of one school where the good-night story had to be told after the children had gone to bed. After a twelve-hour day of activity—without any noticeable intermission—half of them would fall asleep when they gathered around the story teller, so it was found easier and simpler all around to have the children go to bed after their wash and then have the story teller go to the dormitory with them. Sex precocity was no problem in that school. It was not solved because of the unusual wisdom of special technique of the adults in charge; it was because of the normal, active lives of the young and the normal active lives of the grown-ups. A very few cases of sex practice were overcome by the natural living and the lack of secret or hidden places to play in. Proper diet, cleanliness, regularity of living and not too much rest. After the dormitories were cleaned, they were closed until bedtime. Too much rest is a breeder of mischief. Change of activity should provide all the rest that normal, healthy bodies require.

I visited a school in the country that was situated in very beautiful surroundings: great hills and valleys, inviting space around, a brook, not very broad, but full of interest. I spent the night there and arose early the next morning to explore. After a long walk full of beauty and surprises, I returned to the school building. Not a child or teacher in sight. Breakfast was at eight o'clock so I had time for another stroll. I mounted a steep hill to the summit and then descended, calculating that I would reach the house in time for breakfast. Only a few grown-ups were meandering about the grounds, but no boys or girls were in sight. I knew that a number of them were sleeping in tents. I could see the tents but there was no sign of activity. I made my way over to the camp site. As I approached one of the tents a dog barked. It seemed that some teachers occupied that tent. I passed on and finally reached a large tent with a number of cots. Boys from fourteen to sixteen years of age were there with heads as well as bodies buried under the bed clothes. Later I saw that they wore their pants and sweaters in beds. I laughingly made some remark about their lying in bed so late on such a fine morning. One of the boys said, "It isn't our fault. We are not allowed to get up before the rising bell rings." I asked why and the answer was that they would disturb the teachers. The teachers were quite removed from the tent occupied by the boys. The boys could easily have left their tent without troubling their teachers unless the dog notified them. Such a rule was not only stupid, it was vicious. Its reaction on the boys and the school as a whole demonstrated it.

When children are addicted to self-abuse, they are unsocial and ungracious. I suppose they feel that they have to be on the defensive. The earmarks were shown in those boys. They were boorish and unfriendly when they were addressed.

Taking hikes with teachers is not exploring. Teachers are always trying to turn the hike into cultural and academic values. Children are usually suspicious that teachers have something up their sleeves when they suggest outdoor activities. For example, a child once told me he hated the idea of hiking because he would have to write a composition about it the next day.

If those boys were under obligation to stay in bed until they were permitted to rise they at least could not be restrained from investigating their own bodies. When that curiosity is aroused, when they have discovered a gratification from physical contact with their own bodies, the secret practice becomes a difficult problem for the individual and the morale of the school. The difficulty, I feel sure, can be avoided by encouraging the child to arise as soon as he is awake, a thing every child is inclined to do and will do unless interfered with. I have known parents who prevailed on their children to lie in bed late on Sundays and holidays because they themselves wished to lie late in bed. If nothing more serious than forming a lazy habit developed that is serious enough to condemn it; but in nine cases out of ten, sex practices follow in its wake.

I was told by an inmate of a well-known children's hospital that she did not believe there was a child in the place who was not addicted to self-abuse. The nurses were well aware of the fact but felt impotent to deal with it. The woman assured me that some nurses encouraged the practice because it kept the children quiet.

It has also been discovered that nurses in private families very often initiate children into such practices. Children are sure to be quiet and the maids are not bothered with the demands of active, assertive children.

There are many high-priced schools established throughout the country by physicians to try to restore such children to normality. A teacher in one of those schools told me many sad facts of charming children whose lives were one round of daily torture.

The endeavor to control the child necessitated constant supervision and correction. The children had to be kept occupied all through their waking hours and at night their hands were strapped together. The physical, mental and spiritual anguish cannot be imagined. They were sacrificed on the altar of quiet as surely as any sacrificial offering in the past.

Clear the road for the child to live adventurously, even if it is ugly to your sight and discordant to your ears. Let the child risk, dare and attempt, even if he fails to reach somewhere or be someone that he can recognize as related to his own impulsive needs.

Adults are the cause of children's abnormality. Let them turn their attention in upon themselves and no longer distract themselves by trying to find remedies for childish acts. The more remedies they find, the more estranged they become from child life.

CHAPTER SIXTEEN

Toys

The anticipated joy with which a child greets a new toy and the child's savage reaction to the toy after he has had it in his possession a short time, must surely indicate an underlying cause. Every virile child shows the same attitude towards commercial toys, so it seems safe to conclude that the child's eagerness to possess, and the speedy recoil, reveal that there must be something in the very nature of the toy which fails to satisfy the need of the child. If we were alive to the real demands of human life these outbursts would serve to interpret to adults what the child is trying to find out and what the child is striving to say concerning the basic requirements of its own life.

The child seems to want everything that we offer to him but he soon indicates that he has no need for everything presented. The only way that the child can determine his true need is to accept the object, subject it to a test, and thus determine which are useful and which are useless to him.

To any close observer of child behavior, it is evident that the child has an infallible technique which enables him to appraise the forms of life surrounding him, whether organic or inorganic. No artificiality or humbug is proof against it. We all shrink with a sense of unworthiness when the child exercises that power against us personally. Instinctively we feel that the child has penetrated below the surface of our being. The child makes no aggressive attack on us, it simply rejects the spurious offering we have made. This divining rod of the *young* child aids the child in a diminishing degree during its growth clear up to adolescence. As soon as the individual can sense consequences, he begins to estimate the value of material possessions, and so his own developing need separates him from his former pure psychic state. The individual's own growth compels him to face around and struggle in an alien world alone, sensitive to all kinds of extraneous influences.

I have observed that the toy that the child reached for or begged for yesterday is found in a few hours or a few days at most, abandoned or a mutilated wreck. The infant begins its experiment by banging or biting the object, then throwing it on the floor and crying to have it restored, only to renew the attack. Such actions are usually ascribed to the child's inability to recognize the value of the toy. Sometimes such actions are declared naughty and the child's hands may be slapped to emphasize the elder's displeasure. The child can put up no defense, it is unable to answer the "see what you have done" because it does not understand the compelling urge behind the action. The child's response told the story and told it with vigor and decision. Why are we grown-ups unable to interpret the act of the child?

The child reached out for what he instinctively believed was life and received in return an inert, inanimate thing. At once the young child starts to examine it as if he felt there must be a living cause within the outer form. The child soon finds out that the toy is either hollow or stuffed, that it has one set expression that never varies. The doll is just a doll with a fixed smile. When the eyes are gouged out, there is a hollow space which tells the child that the eyes are fake.

The child had no part in the creation of such objects, so the outcome is disappointment, irritation, confusion. I am well aware that many examples may be brought forward to confute my claim. "We have noticed the attachment little boys feel for their toys and that little girls feel for their dolls."

I have studied similar cases and my conclusion is that boys and girls often affect an attachment because of the special attention their toys give them when displayed to their elders and their playmates. We are all familiar with the show-off attitude of children when they are bidding for attention. Toys that had not seen the light of day for months are dug out. As soon as the child discovers that the interest of his elders are no longer centered on his acting, the toy is discarded and the child assumes his normal activities.

I recall the effect of toys on a boy of seven whose mother died during Christmas. Friends of the family vied with one another in loading John with expensive mechanical toys. John showed great exhilaration when the toys were presented to him. His life had been rather simple up to this point. He went from one toy to another but each toy required mechanical skill to operate it. John grew very excited as the day wore on because he began to find out that the intricacies of the mechanism were too much for him. The toys required the attention of an adult. The adults grew tired working over the difficulties so John ended the day in a feverish, fretful, complaining state. John's tension was relieved at bed time by a fit of crying. Night closed in on a day of torture for John.

I did not see John with the toys again nor did I ever hear him speak of them. I surmised that the toys created in John a mental revulsion because they were instrumental in giving him a sense of inability. No doubt, in due time the toys were relegated to the attic or cellar as so much junk. To John they were junk from the start.

I had occasion to see a boy of five almost every day. John's experiences were repeated in a different way in George's life. The grounds in the rear of George's house, were strewn with all sorts of toys; some firmly imbedded in the ground. If they were collected they would furnish a small toy shop. Iron trucks and engines of various sizes, animal toys of all descriptions. In the corner of the porch there was a large expensive toy automobile. There were so many pieces of carpet piled on top of the car that one could see it had been out of use for some time.

But George had three dogs for playmates. One morning I found George with a bird dog that was chained to a tree. Nearby George placed a barrel on its side and propped the barrel on each side so that it would not wobble. George was trying to induce the dog to go into the barrel but the dog refused. He seemed chagrined because the dog would not obey him, so he showed me all the good points of the dog, his long silky ears and hair and especially the dog's curls. George was finding out that the dog had a life of its own. He had a living playmate which could not be treated as a thing. George felt that there was a mutual tie between them. They had many things in which they shared. They could run together and they could be quiet together. Psychologically they understood each other. I think George showed good judgment when he selected the dog and discarded the mechanical toys.

Recently I visited a school where the children were free to initiate their own play work. I found a group of children, ages 8 to 14, seated on some boards laid on a wooden trestle. They were playing taking an air flight; the aviator working away at his imaginary wheel and the rest of the children, calm and relaxed, seemingly enjoying their flight. The plane was halted and a boy, supposedly the pilot, got underneath the plane to adjust some part of the machinery. The pilot soon resumed his place and off they flew again. That play lasted over half an hour.

After that they took the plane apart and the same material was converted into a cage. The children turned themselves into animals and walked into the cage where they were confined. The educator, who was the rallying center of this group of children, kept herself some distance away from the activity.

I felt that there was much more than imaginative play in what these children were doing. They were creative. Form was not static with them. They freely evolved a form and just as freely dissolved the form when their creative needs required it. Children will pretend to be steam engines and automobiles. They will imitate the sounds created by the motion of the different machines. They will play horse in the same way, rearing, snorting and racing, living out spiritually as well as physically and mentally the creature they are portraying. A child goes astride of a stick and gallops off. That same stick he may later convert into a sword or a gun. The child builds up through these simple means the state and condition in himself necessary for the understanding of the things which attract and interest him and which his stage of development and consciousness requires.

The child cannot realize his fundamental needs through any fixed toy. A steam engine is just a steam engine, a doll is just a doll. No serious child, and they are all serious, would try to make a doll or a horse out of a toy engine nor a toy engine out of a doll.

Fixed toys are too limited for a child's creative use. They do not correspond to his own flexible spirit, consequently they distract the child away from simple to complex things.

Toys are not designed for children. They are designed to attract purchasers. The toy maker is dependent on the appeal the toy has for the adult. The absurd and grotesque often amuse adults, so such toys are frequently bought for children because adults are prone to think that the child will react in the same way and will be equally amused. It is easy to discover that that does not always happen.

In my experience the child seems to be immune from foolish exhibitions. He does not see or feel objects in the same manner as his elders. I recall the laughter of adults over some silly trifle and I have seen the child present looking in amazement at the adults. This state of the child is often attributed to lack of development or of humor, but I feel sure it is because of the child's serious approach to the external, which excludes fantastic and ludicrous things.

Commercial toys may be taken as symbols of the present stage of human consciousness. How many realize today that their outer lives should be necessitated by an inner need? The intense diversion which surrounds us all tends to distract the individual from any inner realization. Tabloids, movies, phonographs, radios and the automobile serve to exaggerate the importance of the external life. The reaction of man to all this is a sense of emptiness, loneliness and discontent.

When grown-ups appreciate the child's needs, the making of

commercial toys will prove unprofitable. Even if "My child loves to go to the toy shop," it must not be overlooked that children readily respond to any idea that will promise relief from their feelings of nothingness. The majority of children have been fed on suggestion, surprise and expectation. They consequently react to such feeding excitedly and yet are thoroughly dissatisfied and unhappy.

CHAPTER SEVENTEEN

Music in Education

In a general way I had always had an appreciation of music as it was related to the individual, to the home and to society, just as I valued books and pictures. Many years had to pass, however, before I had any true grasp of the special significance of music in the developing life of humans. How inescapably man is affected by it and even controlled by it; how unconsciously he responds to it from infancy to old age, required many years of observation and thought.

Long before the human being is moved by melody, he is influenced by beat and rhythm.

These psychological discoveries are so many academic statements until experience in one's own life corroborates them. When they are understood, educators will realize how well equipped they are to ward off aggressive assaults of humans whether young or old. Prohibitory rules will fall into disuse when the infallibility of music is recognized, disorder will be transformed into order, the untimely into the timely.

On the crowded New York streets I observed how the music of the hurdy-gurdy changed the movements of the crowd. Even our voices were affected, our speech was modified and influenced by the time, rhythm and melody. People who "before the band began to play," were elbowing and shoving their way along, were subdued by the music of the street organ and began to move in step to the beat of the music. Rhythmically we walked in and around others instead of walking into them. We ceased to be a mob. We were humanized and united to others in an emotional, responsive way.

Discussing this incident with a musical friend, he laughingly related his personal experience with a street organ. He had occasion to transact some business on the lower East Side and as it was a sultry day, he decided to walk leisurely instead of taking a car. He was so absorbed in his own thoughts that he neither noticed nor paid attention to a hand organ which struck up a lively Sousa march. Unconsciously my friend fell into step. When he reached a street that took him beyond the strains of the music he found himself all wrought up emotionally and bathed in perspiration. Annoyed at his overheated state and limp collar, he was, however, able to appreciate what a common hurdy-gurdy could do to him. Previous to that, he had been so occupied in creating and producing music to react on others that he was unaware that he too might be controlled and subjected in the same manner.

In all congregations of people music is a uniting factor. Incongruous elements will, under its influence, resolve themselves into an harmonious whole. Politicians, intuitively, employ music to jolly the crowd.

After these observations I ventured to experiment with the children in the kindergarten. When the children were very noisy and it was difficult to get their attention I would go to the piano and quietly strike one note, repeating the same note until I had their attention. When I saw that they were looking at and listening to me I would close the monotone with the chord. I have had many assistants who experimented with the piano to get attention, but they never succeeded because they struck the note too commandingly, too arbitrarily. They might as well have clapped their hands or rapped on the table.

The imperative quality in music never antagonizes because it is impersonal. Consequently when educators call it to their aid they must feel and express that special quality.

They tell us that everything in the universe, whether organic or inorganic, has its tone note. When that tone is sounded, the reply or echo is audible to all who listen. Therefore it cannot be dismissed as fanciful or speculative to claim the same for every human being. Find out the human's tone note and you will find yourself spiritually *en rapport*. Music is one of the potent factors in the development of the individual. Every message can be conveyed through it. Dalcroze demonstrated how far-reaching is its power even in things seemingly very far removed.

In connection with my kindergarten club there was a mother's club of between forty and fifty women from the neighborhood tenements. The activities of their children often provoked quarrels among the mothers. One night, before the meeting, one mother called me aside and related all the details of a dispute with another mother over her daughter, Nellie, and the other mother's Mary. The disagreement had developed into a real fight. She told me how Mary's mother grabbed her by the head and pulled out a handful of hair. To prove her story she opened her purse and showed me the wad of hair safely packed into her purse. I was apprehensive of the outcome because both women were present at the meeting. I feared that it might break out again. I assumed a calmness that I did not feel. We went through our usual program, which ended with dancing. The dances were generally a few round dances ending with quadrilles and lancers. The piano was so arranged that I could get a good view of the dancers. To my astonishment and alarm I saw the two enemies in the same quadrille and facing corners. Of course they had to embrace when they turned around in the dance. "There might be an outbreak!" But no, they turned around like all the others. What a blessed forgetfulness of the hair-pulling. The sound, beat and rhythm of the music overcame the many days of hate and rage that preceded the dance. I cannot think of anything else that would have been potent enough to subdue their animosity toward one another. I have noticed that when people dance together they are gracious toward one another. Even when the rhythm of the dance is broken by a mistake or an awkward movement it is met with a good-humored laugh. Even the equilibrium of the baby is restored by patting him rhythmically on the back.

I once found myself connected with a group of children who

had come from ultra-radical homes. They had acquired an exaggerated idea of their own importance. Their principal occupation was monopolizing every available opportunity and striving to center attention on themselves. They did not seem to function as social human beings. They were so busy hindering others that they had no time to create. To be unnoticed seemed to them like extinction. The more obtuse ones tried to distinguish themselves by walking on the roof of the new school building, breaking the window glass, mutilating the trees, defiling the brook and swimming pool. It was considered quite a lark to throw broken bottles and glass into the pool. Everything that was to be commonly shared seemed to them profane and tempted them as a target. Freedom to them meant "liberty to do as I please." When their claim was disputed, they followed it up with force. Of course, in time such untamed unrelated elements could be quelled by a firm resolute will. But I realized that along with that there was something else needed. Something that would get beneath the skin of the brute and penetrate to the spirit. Its quality would have to express strength without retaliation, something that would make an impersonal appeal. No appeal could be made through words, for these children could meet words with an avalanche of language and argument. They had been so bred on fine phrases and high-sounding words without the actions that should accompany such thoughts that verbal reasoning offered no solution.

Our difficulties were not thought of when we planned a morning assembly. We conceived the idea of inviting the neighborhood families to join in the salutation to the new day, greeting it with song and dance, hoping at the same time that the incongruous elements would be socially united. The parents accepted the invitation gladly and no morning passed without a gathering of adults. Mothers and fathers joined hands with the young and helped to form a great ring, conceived by Froebel as a symbol of unity. The ring also symbolizes interdependence of the group where each one becomes a visible factor which binds or breaks the unity.

The novelty of the assembly amused the most unruly and toughest children. When they discovered that if they entered the auditorium noisily and let the door bang behind them it did not hinder, even though it disturbed, the singing or dancing in the ring, the wind was taken out of their sails. They came to the assembly to mock, but slowly and reluctantly they yielded to the influence of the music.

One overgrown boy had so cultivated all that was perverse in his nature that he seemed incapable of responding to any form of beauty. The most trivial and insignificant happening he would report in the foulest language. I often suspected that he did it expecting to be rebuked, and in that way find an excuse for more rowdyism. His language was received as if it were normal English. To enter a room quietly seemed to him equivalent to carrying a white flag. Spasmodically he showed that he was weakening. He bolstered his former position by trumping up false charges made against him and then defending by argument his former position in the neighborhood. In the meantime each morning, when he entered the auditorium, he was met by the symbol of unity, the circle, and was greeted with music in song and rhythm. When he realized that he had no power to break up the united group he commenced to make overtures that would in some way find favor for him. He was free to stay outside if he was unwilling to participate. He was free to stay in the room without active participation if he desired. His state of consciousness, however, seemed to require that whatever went on he had to be a recognized part of it. After months of conflict and struggle, it came to pass that the door was opened and closed quietly and he could be seen walking on tip-toe. Through the persistent appeal of music, his offensive obscenity became just ordinary vulgarity.

It was pathetic to see his maimed, distorted sense of power succumb to his real inner nature. He was so weak and helpless under the bluff exterior. All the previous years, seemingly wasted, of his life could not be reclaimed. Habits were formed which contended with his feeble social instinct. He was handicapped with a cumbersome physical body which could not easily respond to an inner demand. He had a man's body with an infant's consciousness. In his changed state, however, there was no loss. An infant's consciousness may seem pathetic when we attempt to measure consciousness, but any degree of awakening has potentiality for expansion and growth. Even a child's soul in a man's body can modify and influence the expression of the body. With occasional outbreaks he grew into an inoffensive, unnoticed member of the neighborhood. This change lifted a burden and annoyance off the community. Others may have called it the development of the sense, but I had the opportunity to observe and study him more intimately than others and I am sure that it was the call of music which he heard and heeded.

In my own experience I recall an incident that left an indelible impression on me. I felt very much wronged and deceived by the action of a minor to whom I was guardian. The child had great musical gifts and I had at considerable sacrifice placed her with a high-priced teacher for violin instruction. The child was told to inform her teacher that she would not begin another term at the close of the present one. It was explained that I could not afford any more instruction that season. When I inquired how the teacher responded to the message I was told that he was unwilling to have the lessons interrupted, and that he would be willing to teach without charge until the summer vacation, which would be in another month.

Reflecting over the teacher's proposal, I wrote to him telling him that I did not feel comfortable about accepting it, and preferred to have the lessons stopped until the fall term. The teacher was in the same neighborhood, so he called to talk it over and I learned from him that he had not made any such offer.

I felt hurt and outraged by the child's deception. The child was present when the teacher called. When he left she went to her room. I went to the basement to do some housework and at the same time to think over how I should meet and treat the situation. She was on the top floor playing, and playing as I had never heard her perform before. Such tragedy, such pathos. I was left limp as a rag. I could not resolve, determine or execute anything. I felt her contrition through her music. No more was needed. She had told her story through music and I was made human by it.

When the human is at war with himself, hopelessly decentralized, music will restore him to the permanent, the spiritual condition.

CHAPTER EIGHTEEN

Reading and Education

When we endeavor to fit a child's conduct into an esthetic form, we create in him a feeling of inferiority, of insecurity and general misdirection. In trying to fit him in, we make of him a misfit. The child's active life, interrupted by the reading habit, is not outgrown; it is just held in abeyance, unrealized, unfulfilled.

When the child transfers his interest to newspaper reading, which is the common literature of most homes, the only things he can understand or respond to are the active, daring incidents which are given first place in newspapers. They attract him as something done, not thought. They appear vital and dynamic to the child. They feed his imagination and appeal to his mind, so it is not surprising if he models his own life after the defiant figures which the newspapers report so prominently. The conventionalities which serve to hedge in the active impulse of the young create a restive spirit of rebellion which predisposes him to tales of revolt because he is in a similar state caused by too much restriction in the home, school and society.

The child has very little opportunity in his environment for adventure and the consequences that follow adventure, so he is unprepared to appreciate that reckless doings may react on the individual life disastrously. He laughs at warnings for he is inclined to think that they are given to frighten him off, like the bogey man of his infancy. As the child advances toward adolescence stocked up with suppressed desires and unrelated ideas, it does not require much prophecy to foretell what he will express as he attains greater freedom of opportunity.

Dr. Miriam Van de Water, in her account of delinquency, states that the featuring in newspapers of divorce, seduction, assault, kidnapping, robbery and murder familiarizes the adolescent with crime and inclines youth to think that adult life is principally made up of such escapades. The lurid accounts suggest danger and excitement, and frequently an inexperienced youth falls into step and in his ignorance often oversteps the adventures he has read about. Immature minds are not qualified to comprehend the serious, thoughtful reports which may sometimes be found in the editorials or special articles in newspapers, so they do not bother with them. Adults are alarmed when an adolescent starts to dramatize the thoughts and ideas he has formed of life, particularly when he makes a strut against society and involves himself with the law. The adult has more concern about exposure and outward consequences than over the spiritually unrealized state of the boy or girl which left them unprotected, unfortified and ignorant of the nature of their primary needs.

There are no real delinquent boys and girls; there are boys and girls physically over-developed, mentally over-stimulated and spiritually famished. Their so-called delinquent experiences are no more a part of them than the feverish newspaper accounts were. They do not know how to satisfy their unrest caused by their spiritual hunger, so they plunge into all kinds of excesses to deaden the feeling which they do not understand.

I am inclined to think that there would be no spiritual unrest if the human being had a normal outlet on the early physical plane which would prepare the way for a gradual normal maturation of the inner life. It would be recorded in every outer manifestation, and could serve to enlarge the life of man from infancy to childhood, from childhood to youth, from youth to manhood.

When I became convinced that application to reading and the acquirement of words reacted unfavorably to the physical body and to the inner life of the individual, I very zealously set to work to counteract its influence. I referred to the thoughts and facts emphasized in books as past thoughts, past achievements which might serve a use when they were needed for exchange, for reference confirmation, corroboration or enjoyment, but no book should be allowed to overlay the search of the individual for further disclosures and discoveries.

In fact, the truths set forth or the facts recorded must be endorsed and supported by man's own experience before man can appreciate or understand them. Words become living agencies as soon as they express the thing which we know to be true. The words of the writer may be used to convey a live thought, a spiritual message, but we are unprepared mentally and spiritually, there is no thought exchange or spiritual message transferred to us. Look, observe, think and assimilate and thus create your own book.

Each individual has a message to deliver; let us get busy with our own lives. Reading is like visiting; sometimes edifying, sometimes wasteful, sometimes helpful.

When the lonely thinker finds that an author has given substance to his own obscure thoughts, he has achieved a union which encourages him to believe and trust in his inner self and the manifestation outwardly of that self.

The one thing we have to bear in mind is that the individual must have realized through his own experiences the things expressed by a writer and thinker or else the words and phrases become decorative, extraneous trappings that clog and betray the spiritual life of man. When the individual understands that his thought separates him from the mass thought surrounding him, he frequently questions the value of the thought which so isolates him. But when he finds a writer who voices the same sentiments, he is then strengthened and confirmed. He regains self-confidence; he knows that he is not a victim of a delusion. It is a dynamic response to a dynamic idea.

Books with a message must touch lives that are prepared for the message. Books for entertainment must reach the one who is seeking amusement or the entertainer bores the reader. In every instance, whether the matter in books be serious or humorous, it must find a correspondent state of consciousness in the reader or the purpose of the author is not fulfilled. Even though the thought of the author is seemingly fixed and permanent on the printed page of a book, the words do not always convey the same meaning to the reader. The meaning is dependent upon the state of consciousness which we bring to the book. Some days we are inspired; some days we are sustained by the message and some days there is no message, no spiritual confirmation for us.

I am inclined to think if we read less we might think more deeply, be more receptive to simple truths. We might even attain more leisure to appreciate the things which live and develop in the outdoors. We might in time find a correspondence and assurance from the life in the open which would enrich and renew our belief in life. We might even get a view of the heavens.

We are suffering today from a pseudo-intellectual obsession. We may hope to free ourselves when we are ready to separate the real from the unreal. The reality from the appearance.

CHAPTER NINETEEN

Adolescent Youth

After long association with children below eight years of age, I found myself in contact with children of mixed ages, i.e., from 2 1/2 to 14 years at the Neighborhood Playhouse and Workshop. We had discarded the idea of education as guiding, teaching or training. The children who came to us did not expect to be prepared for anything, not even for life. We regarded the children as human, living entities with inherent power to expand and develop into self-consciousness as naturally as they had passed from infancy into childhood, from childhood into boyhood and girlhood and from that state into youth. We had confidence that youth would unfold into manhood in the same ratio.

The name indicated that there would be no school, high school or college preparation. Just a playhouse and a workshop for the neighborhood. This simplified our relation with the children, young and old, and also with the parents. There were no tuition fees so the budget was never threatened by the removal of a child and we were never tempted to make concessions on account of finances. We had children from all the social classes surrounding us. Children from well-to-do families, children from tradesmen's families and children from the social outcasts (who lived in the shanty on the fringe of the neighborhood). A woman of comfortable means, with four daughters in the Playhouse, never hesitated a moment over the intimacy of her daughters with all the children. This spirit influenced the other parents, so we had a healthy background for our educational center.

The door was never locked during the day. The children stayed in the Playhouse for as long or as short a time as they wished. Their interests were divided between in door and outdoor activities and attractions. Some days they were indoors most of the day and some days hardly at all.

One year, in the early spring, I observed that the older boys, from 9 to 14 years, were unusually active. A boy would open the door and shout to one or more boys to come out; or they would be gathered in the carpenter shop laughing and talking in low voices over some story or project. Suddenly they would march out of the Playhouse as though their project were perfected. (In other words, they seemed to go into a huddle.) During that period the Playhouse seemed to be used only as a meeting place where they could concoct and hatch their plans. We elders made it a point of conduct not to invade or worm ourselves into the confidence of the boys. If they needed us, they would turn to us in their own good time.

Later on I learned that the Playhouse boys had made warfare on a cave belonging to some boys just beyond our neighborhood. Many things were carried away and destroyed. Reprisals followed which kept stimulating each group to new hostilities. Finally there was a cessation of hostilities. Quiet followed, the boys settled down; the experience seemed to have been worked out.

Fritiof (pronounced Free-tchoff), the leader of the gang, was fourteen years of age. One day he was waiting in the Playhouse for some of the boys. We were alone. I diplomatically introduced the cave incident. I asked Fritiof why they had interfered with the other boys' cave. Fritiof looked abashed and confused but answered, "I don't know, Aunty, why I did it."

Of course he did not understand the invasive urge, but I should have understood it, if I had been in any degree fitted to be his educator.

Fritiof obeyed the impulse that has been manifested all through the ages and all through life. It has been outgrown individually but not racially.

When the adventure of invasion is recorded in legend and myth, including the Old Testament, our vision is not blurred. We have a better perspective because we are not immediately affected. We call such adventures heroic. As soon as such acts are perpetrated in our own vicinity or even in our own time, we fail to focus truly.

I felt it then and firmly believe it now that it is unwise to probe a child for the motive of his act. The youth has no reason that seems good for doing the thing even though he may put up an argument when he is pressed for an explanation. The compelling impulse, which youth obeys, is followed by no apparent remorse. He yields to the call of his impulse and ignores rules and laws laid down by man or society. He regards them as restrictive or limiting. The youth's invasive acts will introduce him into experience that will serve to develop his consciousness of his true relation to society and to himself, in their own time.

Shortly after the cave incident Fritiof announced that he, with his followers, was going to build a house high up in a tree on the playhouse grounds. To be a member one had to shinny up a suspended rope which swung from the platform of the tree house. Only one girl was daring enough or interested enough to attempt it and she did it easily. Fritiof seemed to think it a nuisance to have a girl among them. Fritiof, at this period, gave no indication of interest in girls. Fritiof confided to me one day that he thought they (the gang) ought to forage for their food as long as they had their own house. I asked him where they expected to find anything growing around that they could eat.

"Why, yes, Aunty, there's a whole field of good stuff over at the Italian's."

I thought I understood what was moving in the boy but hypocritically, I asked (also because I feared the censure that I knew would follow the act), "But Fritiof, do you think it would be right for you to take things from a man's garden? That man is dependent on the produce to support his family."

Fritiof fidgeted for a while, seemed uneasy and puzzled then stammered out, "Yes, Aunty, I know, but—"

That "but" revealed an urge more compelling than my moralizing. Fritiof did not understand the urge so could not explain it. Am I advocating that he should go scot free? No indeed! but his reaction should come directly from the farmer. Fritiof needed reaction, not preaching.

A few days after my talk with Fritiof I heard a "Hoo, hoo! Hoo, hoo!" repeated many times. I went to the veranda to see what it meant. There was Fritiof with his followers coming across the fields. Fritiof and the others were in high humor, as he flourished some heads of lettuce.

I felt flattered that they were willing to include me in their adventure, but I, at the same time, shrank from the criticism that would be directed against the new experiment in education. Our critics might even charge that we encouraged the boys. However, our allegiance belonged with the young. I was confirmed in the belief that the boys were living out their boyish needs in the eternal way. We did not decree it thus, so we would hold life responsible for the impulse, suggestions and compelling urge which all the young reveal.

One day Fritiof was obliged to go into town on an errand for his father. Willie, the next older boy, had to assume responsibility. When Fritiof returned he found Willie, brushed and combed, and all dressed up in his best suit, with a tie. The rule in Fritiof's gang was to wear overalls. Fritiof upbraided Willie, called him a shirk and a dude; then he followed up his disapproval with, "I know why you came down from the tree and got dressed up. Mabel's here. You know very well what kind of girl Mabel is. I wouldn't mind if it was any other girl. You know the way she treated John."

Fritiof did not explain how Mabel had treated John, but the boys seemed to understand. Willie tried to defend himself. He protested that he had not dressed for Mabel: "I felt like taking a bath, I was so hot."

"Well, why did you put on a tie and brush your hair?" asked Fritiof. "You can't belong to this club unless you take off those clothes and put on your overalls."

Willie, torn between conflicting emotions, walked away A few minutes later he appeared in his overalls. He revealed that, at his stage of development, adventure was stronger need than the companionship of the opposite sex.

One evening the children of the locality were congregated in a vacant lot next to the Playhouse, swapping stories about firemen, baseball players and fighters. A wagon loaded with soft drinks stopped at one of the houses. The driver went around to the back of the house to deliver something, when suddenly Fritiof jumped on the wagon and snatched a bottle of soda water. Barrett, one of the boys, left the group and came over to where I was standing. He had a fine appearance and was much better mannered than Fritiof. However, his advantage was only in externals. Barrett had many mean traits and was cowardly to boot. Barrett started to tell me what Fritiof had done. "I'm going home," he added. "The first thing you know he'll be arrested."

I regarded what Fritiof had done as another adventure: I also knew why Barrett was going home; not because he had any compunction about drinking the stuff, but because he was afraid of being mixed up in any consequences. I said, "Well, Barrett, don't think yourself any better than Fritiof. Do you remember when you went into the cellar of the Playhouse and took many things away? You sneaked into the cellar while Fritiof openly took the bottle of soda. Don't be too self-righteous." Barrett looked chagrined but quickly made for the safety of the house.

When the driver returned he mounted his wagon, whipped up his horses and quickly drove away. He did not stop to examine his stock and no one snitched on Fritiof.

The next morning the mother of a boy named Mark came to the Playhouse to talk about Fritiof. She was determined to remove Mark if Fritiof or his brothers and sister were permitted to continue at the Playhouse. She cited the garden incident and now the wagon affair settled the matter. She would be afraid to let Mark associate with Fritiof.

Mark had never had a chance to find himself because his capable mother controlled every action that she could find out about. We were sorry to part with Mark but we would feel much worse over Fritiof. Fritiof's conduct made us reflect and ponder. There was growth in associating with Fritiof. With Mark everything was pleasant, polite and conventional, but no expression. Neither Mark nor anyone else could understand the depth or height of Mark's nature so long as he was constantly directed.

A few days after the interview with Mark's mother, I learned that the family used to open the outlet of their cesspool every night to let the water flow into the gutter. This was proscribed and forbidden by the health authorities, but it was a common practice in that well-to-do suburb. Within a few months, Mark's father was sent to Sing Sing for promoting fake bonds.

The bottle taken off the wagon seemed to round out the impulsive, boyish acts of Fritiof. It seemed to close an epoch. I did not mention the incident to Fritiof and he did not refer to it. The change in him was very marked. He dropped his leadership in the gang and became thoughtful and serious.

One evening Fritiof appeared all dressed up; new hat, suit, a fancy tie and a pair of tight patent-leather shoes. He tried to feel at ease but also seemed to be half ashamed. I felt that he wanted to show himself to me but I hesitated to say anything. Finally I told him how well he looked. "But," I smiled, "aren't the shoes a little too tight?"

"Oh! these aren't tight, Aunty, they are just comfortable."

I tried to cover up my mistake by saying, "I suppose they look tight because they fit so smoothly." I could see David Copperfield's and my own youth's feet in Fritiof's.

At this stage of his development, Fritiof seemed to have turned his back completely on his former escapades. He was more courteous toward the girls but also shy and reserved with them. Many overtures were made by the girls to him but he did not respond to their advances. He seemed, to me, to look at things and people more sentimentally. One evening a hand organ was playing in neighborhood. Fritiof was very quiet for a while, then when I hear music." I wondered if he were lonely for his past, boyish, carefree life. I almost wished he was back there again.

The road which he had entered on now had, no doubt, its compensations, but it seemed lonely and unfamiliar. He had to face this road alone. In his boyhood he had the company and loyalty of the gang. That way was behind him never to be retraveled. Fritiof had completed the cycle of his boyhood needs. He was well qualified physically, mentally and spiritually for his new experience. With the development of his emotional life, he responded and tuned himself to music, color and form. His effort to manifest his inner feelings was shown in his dress and his manner toward other humans, and even in his tight patent-leather shoes. He also became less exacting with the boys. He seemed eager to give service to the girls and women. In every way Fritiof demonstrated that he was facing the future with a clean slate.

Later on we moved from Fritiof's neighborhood so I did not have the satisfaction of seeing him develop into manhood. I never doubted, however, that all would be well with him. "As it was in the beginning, so it shall be forever."

In our later educational environment we found ourselves with large numbers of adolescent boys and girls. The background of these boys and girls was more complex. Fritiof's parents were united and they were both deeply attached to their children. Now we were facing the problems of children whose homes were disrupted, whose parents were estranged from each other, or one or the other parent had passed away. Nevertheless in their adolescent state these boys revealed the same signs as Fritiof did. When their emotions were stirred they were reticent, shy and reserved.

Sam, a former member of the colony and the school, had moved away. He used to come back to see Rose. They would sit on a bench on the lawn, Rose at one end and Sam at the other, not even exchanging a word, just satisfied to be in one another's company. Sam frequently came back for the young people's dance but did not dance. He was too shy to dance with Rose and too loyal to Rose to dance with another girl. I used to play the piano for the dancing and Sam spent most of the time at the piano with me, talking around his feelings but never of them. One thing he never forgot was to ask for my hand going home. Rose never revealed in conduct her feelings for Sam, but she too was sure to engage a hand for the trip home. I used to laugh, inwardly, through sheer joy over their innocent security. Sam was often invited to eat at the school but he never accepted.

Two other boys manifested their adolescent state in some sort of daring. They liked to do brave things before boys as well as girls. On the other hand the girls showed a maternal instinct by caring for younger children and also in service for the boys. The girls seemed to find their emotional outlet in interpretative dancing. The boys despised dancing. They would leave the room in disgust as if they were embarrassed by it. Also the girls expressed themselves in painting religious pictures and dramatizing religious subjects. Although they were largely Jewish girls, they painted the Madonna and Christ pictures. This phase invited adverse criticism from a few quarters but we were not disturbed by it.

The girls, like the boys, were enveloped in a cloak of reserve which, I am thankful to recall, we never minded. I have heard adults talking to young boys and girls about their sweethearts, a most unpardonable sin. It outrages the idealistic, abstract emotional feeling of the adolescent. It tears open the reserve and blights the pure feeling. The familiarity coarsens the relationship by concretizing prematurely the vague, intangible feelings of the adolescent.

In my study of the growing boy and girl, it seemed to me as if their regard for one another was more symbolic than actual. In any case it would seem that when growing boys and girls endeavor to keep their feelings to themselves, adults should in decency keep their hands off. The reserve of the adolescents, I believe, protects them from premature manifestations. The first blossoming of their emotions may be an indication, a forerunner, perhaps—very beautiful and dignified—therefore, let us grown-ups see to it that we do not mar it.

On the other hand I have had experiences with boys and girls who never had an opportunity to work off the roughness of their undeveloped state, who never had experienced what it meant to find out, in their own way, what their relationship was to their playmates and society.

The great spiritual clearing-house of the developing child is where he can hear himself talk, where he can feel himself move, where he can see the reflection of his acts, his attempts to alter or to tear down exultingly.

When he has exhausted his crude physical sense of power, he is then fitted to reach inward and find out something of his inner strength. When this state of the child is interfered with his development is postponed. He must outlive the rudimentary physical consciousness or he will carry the crudity of the primitive instincts into every relation of his later life. He must outgrow his barbarism through exhibiting it.

Because of restrictions in infancy, childhood, boyhood and youth, we find such adolescents experimenting with sex on the physical plane. Their adolescence is spent in actualities. Over-familiar in their conduct, obscene in their remarks, their relationship with one another becomes an offense, a stench. Prematurely dealing with forces which they truly never feel, their self-delusion, intoxicates them into expressions which cause an individual loss and a loss to society as a whole.

My experiences have led me to conclude that it is a perversion of the adolescent state when it is divorced from the rhythm of the abstract emotional life and plunged into the actual manifestation.

The adolescent need is to build. If his previous stages of development have been rounded out, i.e., if his early needs have been allowed freedom to show their crudity, thus realizing his power through touching, thwarting, changing and tearing down the forms which surround him, he will build without harshly expressing his adolescent need in physical contact which would be a loss and a blunder in his growth.

The finest achievements of the individual life are rooted in the adolescent period. When a boy or girl normally unfolds into adolescence through a preceding, well-filled-out adventurous stage, they are fitted for the esthetic, abstract qualities of human life. The adolescent state has bequeathed to us religion, music, painting, poetry, color, form.

CHAPTER TWENTY

Children's Emotions

The "Hoboes," a name adopted by a group of boys and girls between the ages of eight and twelve, were on their way home from their weekly gathering. Their assembly was usually a very simple affair lasting one hour, from six to seven P. M. Every moment of that hour had to be carefully planned, so a boy or girl was appointed to look after the program for the evening, which included singing, dancing and games. Usually one or two blood-curdling plays, in which everybody in the play was killed, was included in the program.

I was called the "Aunty" of the "Hoboes" and another teacher was called the "Uncle." The "Aunt" and "Uncle" were to help to further their plans, but in no way to interfere with them. My responsibility was to play for the dancing and singing. The "Uncle's" responsibility was to dance every dance, sing every song and play the villain when they needed a large one.

A few precocious boys and girls who had outgrown the simple routine of the club introduced kissing games with forfeits. The new development interested me. On this particular night kissing games occupied nearly the whole time. I was called into the ring a few times, when some boy or girl was too bashful to call another child. There was one girl who was the center of attraction. Elizabeth, pretty and vivacious, was called into the ring so many times she became the distinguished one in the gathering. Some were lesser favorites but some were not called into the ring at all.

I became absorbed in studying Elizabeth's reaction to so much attention, and I gave very little thought to the neglected children. As we started for home, Alexander, an eight-year-old boy, hurried up to me and asked to have my hand going home. When we walked down the road we found ourselves behind a group of girls who were with Elizabeth, in spite of her being the favorite. After all the kissing, the boys were with their gangs and the girls in their own groups. The gallantry of "seeing the girl home" had not yet developed. The kissing indicated something but that something was still in abeyance, so my mind was at ease.

As we walked along hand in hand, Alexander began to talk about the entertainment and added, "Do you know, Aunty, that I wasn't called into the ring once?"

I told him I had not noticed it. I began to speculate about what it meant to him and how he was affected by being overlooked. Alexander was never a very active social member. He was neither popular nor unpopular with the children, so that might be one reason why he was not called into the game.

Was a desire for social contact aroused? Or was there some sex feeling aroused by the kissing demonstration? I needed time to weigh and consider its significance.

Elizabeth was very flushed and radiant over her triumph. She was too excited to go directly home so she proposed to see another girl home. This would carry her past the homes of a number of other children, including Alexander. I heard Elizabeth's proposal and I thought this would be Alexander's opportunity to be with Elizabeth. So I said, "Alexander, wouldn't you like to go on with the girls who are seeing Nancy home, then you will be able to come back with Elizabeth?" "No," he replied, "I don't need to go to Nancy's house. I've been there lots of times. Didn't you know that?" I had my answer.

He had no need for Elizabeth's company nor the company of any of the other girls. He seemed to be only wondering why he was not included in their game. To him it was merely a game. Socially he was unawakened. He was always so absorbed in his own projects that he paid little attention to what was going on about him.

The following Christmas the children planned to exchange gifts, or some of them did, with one another. Their gifts were anonymously placed at the breakfast plates. Alexander must have heard about it because I was astonished to see him come through the kitchen before the breakfast bell rang, enter the dining room and look at his place. There was no gift for Alexander. He tried to hide his embarrassment; he laughed nervously and quickly left the room as if he were ashamed. I was tempted to place something at his plate but I controlled my feeling, for I believed Alexander needed this experience. It did not occur to him to fetch a gift for another child.

There was no need to preach to Alexander about giving and getting being reciprocal. He was thoughtful enough to get all that he could use from that experience.

The following incident will indicate how difficult it is for the adult to comprehend or appreciate the child's state of consciousness; how repeatedly the child's real need is not recognized. This incident happened in a kindergarten composed entirely of Negro children.

The majority of the little girls had their hair braided and tied with string or well-worn ribbons. One little girl, Mandy, was quite conspicuous with new pink ribbons which distinguished her from the others. Their morning talk, singing and story telling was unusually long this morning. Mandy raised her hand quite a number of times for permission to leave the room. The kindergartner either did not notice Mandy's signal or she may not have considered the need urgent enough to interrupt the exercises.

When Mandy received permission to leave it was too late. Mandy had an accident which overwhelmed her. An efficient attendant bustled Mandy off and gave her the attention she needed. In due time the child and attendant returned to the kindergarten room. Mandy in tears and filled with a sense of disgrace wanted her friend Susie to stay with her. The discipline of the kindergarten, however, was too formal to disturb the "life" groups to which Mandy and Susie, respectively, belonged. Mandy's continuous weeping and the solicitude of all the kindergarten children for Mandy held up every group activity. Their attention could not be diverted from Mandy. Finally the kindergartner in charge of Susie's group, conceded that Mandy might sit beside Susie, but she could not have the privilege of working at anything as long as she insisted on staying with a group to which she did not belong.

I overheard Susie confide to Mandy that when she had finished her mat, which she was weaving, she would give it to her. Still, Mandy was not consoled. Susie then turned to a playmate seated near them and said, "See how Mandy cries and she has such lovely pink ribbons."

Lovely pink ribbons! What a distinction! Just the thing to serve as an antidote to her present disgrace. Mandy had something that no other child present had. Mandy heard Susie and the other children talking about her pink ribbons. Her crying ceased. When Mandy uncovered her face the children greeted her with smiles. The tension in the room was over and the children and Mandy were again on an equal footing. More than equal, because Mandy had a gift from Susie along with those priceless pink ribbons. An unschooled, untutored, unpsychologically-trained child intuitively had restored the poise of Mandy and the whole kindergarten group.

Such a simple thing—pink ribbons! The children could appreciate their value, but the adults were too far removed in their feelings and thoughts to think of such a vanity as holding the solution.

"Except ye become as little children, ye shall not enter the Kingdom."

CHAPTER TWENTY-ONE

Youth's Confidant

After a free and easy talk with young boys and girls, how confident we adults feel that we have lowered the bars and the way is now clear for a frank discussion of their problems, or any problems for that matter, which exist or may arise. The adult feels that he brings to the young a wealth of experience which has matured his knowledge and judgment as to the true value of the common happenings in human life irrespective of age, state or condition. This idea is deceptive and may lead the well-meaning adult father away from youth.

When I try to understand the cause of the dividing line which marks off youth from age, inexperience from experience, I am inclined to believe that the cleavage is necessary and natural. The thoughts and dreams of youth are idealistic and impractical. If they were allotted a place in the adult world they would soon destroy the cherished conventions of adult life. The dynamic spirit of youth is not able to comprehend that within the static patterns of age there are age dreams and age ideals.

The divergent needs erect barriers for protection on both sides. Youth protects its dreams and age its acquirements. Elders have all the evidence on their side; they were once young, they have gained knowledge which they are willing to share with the young and inexperienced. Youth rejects this and starts out to experiment with life as if his elders had nothing stored up which could benefit youth. When age attempts to advise youth, youth feels hindered. Youth is impatient of advice, and I can see the value of this protective attitude against age.

When, however, the adult can demonstrate that he has attained a self-consciousness which enables him to discern that the true values in life are the inner values, it may come to pass that such an adult will be qualified to exchange thoughts with youth. Youth will then find assurance and recognition from its elders in place of the intimidation it now receives.

The relationship that now exists between youth and age prohibits confidence or revelation. The best confidant for youth, I am inclined to think, is one of their own development. Such a person will rejoice and will encourage the project and perhaps suggest ways and means to further it. Instead of sensing danger, as too often elders do, the young are exhilarated by the sense of adventure. Obstacles are brushed aside where one conceives the idea and confides it to his equal. There are now two to execute it. That is what youth is searching for—fulfillment. "There are two of us."

If the project, after it is concretized, proves foolhardy the consequence turns the adventure into an experience which gives knowledge to the originator. I feel sure that the one who merely aided does not derive the same benefit, for he was only a helper not a creator. True experience is the outcome of a creation. I am convinced that we cannot profit by the experiences of others. If the projection of a creative thought does not prove itself according to the inner idea of the creator, the companion who assisted does not connect the failure with himself. If it succeeds he may share outwardly in the triumph but spiritually he is not benefited. He may have helped to execute but it is not given to him to relate spiritually the success or defeat to himself. The experience, the knowledge belongs to the creator.

When the child's elder recognizes how subordinate a relation he holds to the young, when he accepts it as true and desirable, he gains peace of mind himself and thus relates himself with the young on an inner psychic plane, instead of the physical, authoritative plane he formerly held.

The instinct of age is to shield the young from what age thinks is youth's inexperience. Age has no true perspective of the inner life of youth. Age looks on youth's adventures too gravely or too lightly.

Age fails to see the events as part of youth's spiritual needs. Youth's sources, his family or social life, but rarely if ever in connection with youth's own inner self. It may be that only the poet can conceive that a human may fail utterly in his outer relation to himself, to others, and nevertheless realize himself spiritually. "Shall man succeed in that he seems to fail?"

If accidentally youth should express some inner feeling to age the disclosure would likely be followed by dissatisfaction and unrest to both. An experience of a friend of mine who thought aloud to her mother is a very common experience. "Mother," my friend asked, "can you think of any way in which I could improve myself?"

The mother was silent for awhile and then said, "Well, I think if you wore a bustle it would help you."

In conclusion let me say that even when youth proposes—what seems to the adult mind—a dangerous undertaking, youth in the execution of the idea develops resources that were latent in himself and so the risk, if it did exist, is overcome in the execution.

The hidden power, which youth experiences, nullifies the warnings of age, for the thing which might happen doesn't always happen.

APPENDIX A

Elizabeth Byrne Ferm — A Biographical Note

Galva, Illinois was a pioneer town in 1857 when Elizabeth Byrne Ferm (Mary Elizabeth Byrne) was born there on December 9th. Her brother was the second child born in the settlement. Her father had gone there before his wife in order to prepare a living place of some kind, as he expected to go into farming on a large scale. When his young wife arrived and saw the hut that he had built for her, she sat down on the step and vowed that she would not live in such a place. But John Byrne simply said, "Well, if you want to sit out there tonight to meet the bears maybe you'll make their acquaintance." When the gloaming came, she decided that she did not want to get acquainted with the bears.

When Elizabeth was about six years of age, her father suddenly died, and her mother returned to her grandmother's home in Montreal. She remembered that there was a war on but she did not know at the time what it was about. She recalled being on the street in Montreal when the news came that President Lincoln had been shot and that she ran in to tell her mother about it.

Elizabeth received her first schooling in some small private schools and then in the French Convent in Lachine. Her schooling included piano lessons, the practice of which she pursued assiduously for many years. The piano seems to have been her one delight at that time, and she finally studied with Laval, a famous pianist and composer.

When she was about twenty she married Martin Battle, somewhat older than herself, and they came to New York to open a bookstore on Third Ave., near Bloomingdale's drygoods store. Evidently she had a mind of her own and they did not agree about the conduct of the store. After a few years she decided she had made a mistake, and took to teaching and living with some friends, but continued studying the piano at the New York Conservatory of Music from which she was graduated on June 13, 1885.

In the early days of Henry George's Anti-Poverty Society Elizabeth joined the movement and her certificate shows that she became a member on May 16, 1887. She was active also in the Woman's Suffrage Movement and went to the convention in Washington as a delegate when Susan B. Anthony and Elizabeth Cady Stanton were the leaders.

Her mother having moved from Montreal to Brooklyn to be near her daughter, took up her home with Elizabeth. Shortly afterwards Elizabeth's sister came to Brooklyn for special medical care and nursing. She brought her very young son and daughter with her. The sister died after many months of lingering illness, during which time Elizabeth acted as nurse. Instead of sending the children back to their father in Montreal, Elizabeth decided to mother them. To do the job properly she resolved to take a course in child education. She joined the Training School for Kindergartners attached to the Free Kindergarten of Dr. Newton's All Souls' Church under the direction of Miss Mary L. Van Wagenen, from which she was graduated a June 11,1889.

After graduation, she refused numerous offers to do kindergarten teaching as she had her work cut out for her with the care of the household and the two children. She was so highly recommended, however, by her former instructor that about a year after her graduation she was persuaded to take charge of the Brooklyn Guild kindergarten.

She commenced putting into practice the theories she had learned in the training school, and which were based on Froebel's ideas of child education. Initiative or self-activity and creative ability were the qualities that Froebel emphasized in his work, but they were not given first place in the training school because it was easier to teach methods than principles. The pupils should have been told that the methods were given merely to illustrate the principles and were not to be used as devices for "busy work." The devices or methods were fascinating to the kindergartner because of the control it gave her over the children and the feeling of having gotten something from her training.

But Elizabeth had not forgotten how to observe and wonder. While giving the children a lesson in the use of cubes, cylinders, spheres, etc. it occurred to her that the children were merely following her directions and were not using their own minds. She was thinking for them. Was there any benefit to be gotten from mere copying?

She soon came to the conclusion that whatever methods might be used they must not contradict the principles which are summed up in one of Froebel's paragraphs: "But whatever self-evident, living, absolute truth rules, the eternal principle reigns, as it were, and will on this account, maintain a passive, following character. For the living thought, the eternal principle as such demands and requires free *self-activity and self-determination* on the part of man."

Though it was not easy to break away from the set routine of the kindergartner, Elizabeth noticed how the children reacted to the various devices that were used to instruct them rather than to help them express themselves. While trying to keep to the "passive following" of Froebel, she observed that the children were inclined to do the work in their own way in spite of previous instructions. She wondered what would happen if the children were left entirely to their own initiative in the use of the materials.

So, the wools, needles, sewing cards and other "gifts" were left for the children to make their own selections and the cards for sewing designs, which had been pricked to make exact forms, were changed to the soda cracker type so that the children could sew pictures according to their own desires within the limits of the straight lines. The children then originated many new designs more beautiful and varied than those the adults made for them. The variety showed the individuality of the children and verified the statement made by Froebel that each individual is unique and complete in himself. The outer manifestation became a representation of the inner need of the individual, instead of the mere copying of the kindergartner's instructions.

As Elizabeth had not gained an understanding of Froebel's vital ideas from the training school nor the kindergartners whom she met nor the books that she read, she decided to make a study of the children on her own account, by doing what Froebel advises when he said, "Come, let us with our children live."

The result was a constant loosening of the reins on the activities of the children. They not only selected their materials for their work but eventually selected their games; they became self-active. The results were so wonderful that it confirmed her in the belief that the more freedom an individual has the better will he express the innate goodness of life. It had seemed to her that devilishness, mere contrariness, rebelliousness, must be the result of suppression somewhere. Here were demonstrated the results of freedom more wonderful than could have been expected.

It was the usual thing to open the activities in the morning in the kindergarten by having the little chairs placed in a circle so that they could all sing the good morning song together, tell stories and talk about the flowers, the weather, etc. As the chairs were put in their places before the children arrived, it was, by implication, more or less compulsory for the children to take their places in the circle as they arrived in the morning.

One morning two little tots who had been hobnobbing for some days, excluding others from their deliberations, as children will do, decided not to go into the circle that morning. It was a plain case of revolt against authority. Elizabeth was at first nonplussed. Had she not given them so much freedom that they could concede at least this one requirement? Then it occurred to her that the individual can feel but one restriction at a time and why should she be giving them their freedom, when all she should do was to remove hindrances to their freedom. One restriction is as serious as many because the individual feels himself a slave to some one else's desires or demands. After that morning, she decided that the children would not be required to sit in the circle if they decided otherwise, but few of them refrained from joining the circle for they liked the songs and the stories. It was merely requested of the independents that they should not disturb the story telling and the singing.

Some time after Elizabeth resigned from the Guild, Martin Battle, who had been living in Denver, came back to New York a sick man and soon passed on. So we married in September, 1898, and turned our thoughts to the possibility of continuing the work of education by ourselves. We had thought of moving into a neighborhood of many children so that we could have a school or kindergarten of our own in the house.

A friend in Philadelphia, Miss Otis, with four adopted children, induced us to wait a year so she could dispose of her large house, as she wanted her girls to attend our school. Mrs. J. Stanwood Menken persuaded her brother-in-law, S. Levy Lawson, to join with his children. Mr. Lawson and I spent much time in and around New York to find a suitable place and finally located in New Rochelle where we found a large house for Miss Otis, next to a smaller one for the school, and one nearby for the Lawson family. A tenement was in sight a street away which housed a number of children. In order to be free with my time, I resigned from a business position and took up dental prosthesis for a living.

We called the school the "Children's Playhouse." Mrs. Menken supplied money for materials and rent and we gave our time. There was no charge for attendance although most of the parents could afford it. We did not want money to enter into the question of attendance at the "Children's Playhouse." The school was opened on October 1st, 1901.

Before the year was out, however, Mrs. Lawson passed away and as Mr. Lawson found his younger boy, John Howard, settling a dispute with one of the tenement house boys with his fists, he decided to send the boy to a boarding school where he would be brought up according to "Hoyle," so he moved to Yonkers.

Dr. Thaddeus Hyatt wished to join us with his children but could not afford to leave his house in Dyker Heights, Brooklyn. When he got word that we were contemplating moving to some more suitable environment, he came and spent an evening with us. We sat up half the night discussing the matter and he urged us to look up his neighborhood, which he claimed had as democratic an atmosphere as we could wish.

At Dyker Heights we found a house suitable for the "Children's Playhouse" and other houses for the families who went with us to the new neighborhood. Mr. and Mrs. Menken also took a house in the neighborhood. Thus after one year in New Rochelle, we moved to Dyker Heights and opened the school with fifteen or sixteen children. During the year a new building was put up for us for which Miss Otis contributed the money and we moved into a building appropriate for our needs.

Elizabeth had an interesting and happy time at Dyker Heights, holding weekly meetings to which parents came at times to discuss the question of education. Visitors from Manhattan, such as Bolton Hall, Leonard Abbott, and A. C. Pleydell often attended these meetings and Howard Crosby included a chapter on our school called the "American Experiment" in his *Tolstoy as a Schoolmaster*. But before the fourth year, misunderstandings and emotional troubles developed among the parents. Elizabeth became involved because of their habit of bringing their troubles to her. So, after four years in Dyker Heights, although our educational work was not in question, Elizabeth decided to move into a workingmen's neighborhood, as we had originally intended.

In the spring of 1906, we bought a piece of ground for a camp in Newfoundland, New Jersey, to which we took seven children who wanted to live outdoors and sleep in a tent all summer. Elizabeth did the general cooking while the girls made any desserts they wanted from apples and berries gathered by the boys. They all made their own straw beds, swept the tent, tidied up the grounds, and fetched the water as well.

The location of another school was put off until the fall when the children would have gone home. On our return to the city, Elizabeth discovered a vacant store in a tenement on Madison Street which she thought might be a good place to start a kindergarten. The street was teeming with children but the neighborhood was not conducive for an unusual school. I looked the place over and could see that it was not a suitable place to start a school for the growth of the feeling of freedom, as the people were of the orthodox type who would not appreciate such a school. Besides we could get no farther than a kindergarten. But Elizabeth was so enthusiastic about it because of the number children that I finally consented.

We started there in the fall of 1906 and we did the best we could under the circumstances. There was no yard for the children to play in so the next year moved to a store on the next block where there was a yard. We carried on a free kindergarten for seven years until I found I would have to change my work and way of living if I wanted to retain my health. We bought a farm in Connecticut where we made our living for seven years although we had not done any heavy work before. Elizabeth not only kept a house in fine condition but also helped with the garden and the chickens. She even helped to shuck the corn and could do it well.

In 1920, Harry Kelly of the Modern School at Stelton came to plead with Elizabeth to go down to look over the boarding house of the school. He said we could have a free hand and Elizabeth couldn't resist. We arrived at the colony on the evening of April 20, 1920. Elizabeth was then 62 years of age.

We found the house and dormitory in a run down condition with the grounds outside looking like a dump for ashes and the boarding house in debt to the tune of fourteen hundred dollars. Before the summer was over, we had been asked to take over the school as well.

We felt that we must get all this under control and turn it into a home for children before adding the school to our responsibilities. As we preferred doing educational work where we could have complete care and control of the children, as was promised we would have in the boarding house, we feared taking over the school where there would be so many "day" children. We changed the name of the Boarding House to Living House so the children would not get the impression of merely boarding. We wished the children to feel that it was their home.

Shortly after we started our work at the Living House to build it into a home for children, Elizabeth noticed that the small children of the colony had no center of activity and sometimes seemed to be wandering around aimlessly or as if lost for something to do. Being in sympathy always with small children as well as older ones, she offered to open a kindergarten in the old barn if the mothers would get the materials necessary, a list of which she gave them. They gladly went to work to get donations and to make small tables and stools out of old boxes and crates. At nine o'clock one morning in May or June of 1920, the kindergarten was opened with nearly all the children of the colony ready and eager to take part. Not knowing what to expect, since they had not been in a kindergarten or school, they were astonished to find materials with which to do something, with which to create, so they naturally and eagerly went to work.

Curiosity about the innovation kept the older children from going up to their own school; they stood at the open doors of the old barn, diffident about going in to a kids' place. But fascinated by the colors of the wools and beads and the activity, they gradually edged their way into the room and were soon using wools on cards, building with Froebel's gifts, cubes and oblongs, and taking part in other activities of the kindergarten that they had been deprived of when younger.

When Joseph Cohen, the President of the Board of The Modern School, saw activity and order under freedom—no rules, no compunction—he said it was what he had pictured in society and so conceived the idea of having us take over the school as well. Shortly afterwards he induced us to attend a special board meeting at the home of Abe Arnold, an attorney and member of the Board, at which he proposed that we take over the school as co-principals. As we did not believe in the form of school that they had been carrying on—reading, writing, arithmetic and propaganda only, though they had tried art expression with Hugo Gellert as teacher—we demurred and said that we had all that we could do to help the children directly under our care in their educational growth, and besides, we felt that we could not be of much help to day pupils.

But Cohen was a quietly insistent man and suggested that we could have a free hand in changing the curriculum and the use of the school building and addition of any materials that were needed. It was put up to the staff, about seven of them. Would they be willing to co-operate in the new work? They said they would.

At the Labor Day convention in September, 1920, the matter was brought before the members and the question of education was discussed and debated from eight p.m. to two a.m. without pause, after which a vote was taken and we were unanimously elected co-principals.

When we took over the school on October 1st, we changed the class rooms into shops—craft shop for wood and metal work, art shop, print shop, library and study room and later a sewing and weaving room. The large auditorium was used for the kindergarten and the morning assembly.

When we opened the assembly in the morning Elizabeth suggested to the parents that they join in the circle, holding hands with the children to form a large circle, while singing the good morning song and other songs, which Elizabeth introduced while she played the piano. After the singing she played for interpretative dancing in which some of the mothers took part. Not many of the boys had the nerve to try but the girls did some interesting dancing.

For some time we had weekly parents' meetings for the discussion of educational problems, and after two or three years Elizabeth offered to form a class for parents: to meet once a week in order to explain to them the meaning of the creative activity, initiative and self-activity of Froebel's principles.

These were well attended and the mothers took notes, asked questions and wrote small essays on the subjects discussed.

How Elizabeth stood it all was a marvel. She supervised the work at the Living House and took part in it by getting up at five in the morning to get the breakfast ready by seven o'clock, with the help of the older children, saw it that the dining room, kitchen and dormitory were cleaned and put in order, and was up at the school at nine to open the assembly by playing the piano and introducing the songs and then carrying on the kindergarten until 12 o'clock.

She also acted as the "Aunty" of "The Hoboes" on their weekly evening socials at which they played games and acted in impromptu plays, and helped the older girls and boys at their social dances by playing the piano for them.

Her menus were prepared a week in advance and in the evening she often looked over the music for new songs and to prepare her order of songs for the morning, On Saturdays she helped to do the weekly house cleaning. On Sundays she saw many of the mothers who were anxious to have some word with her. Toward the end of our stay, in 1924, and 1925, she played the piano for community singing and folk dancing on Sunday nights, in order to bring discordant elements into harmony, which she seemed to do for the time that the Sunday night gatherings were carried on. Outside influences, however, never cement discordant elements into friendships; that must come from within.

All this activity lasted while Elizabeth was between 62 and

68 years of age, during which time she had to go away for a few months to recuperate.

After five and a half years of strenuous work at the school and Living House, we resigned to go to our place in Newfoundland, New Jersey, where we lived until 1935.

In 1954, Elizabeth had a slight stroke which affected her hand and her speech slightly. After some treatments, she seemed to be as well as ever, at least mentally, and so we were urged to return to the Modern School at Stelton again. We went back in June, 1935.

After a few years of activity at the school, in hurrying home in a storm on a hot day when she refused to ride, Elizabeth reached the house somewhat exhausted. It was characteristic of Elizabeth to go through with what she had undertaken to do, sometimes to her own detriment. She had started to walk so she was determined to do it. The next morning she had another slight stroke which affected her hand again. She decided that she would not attend school any more. She was then in her eightieth year. She still attended to her housework with my help, until she again broke the rules in the care of her health. On June 12th, 1942, I came home at noon to find Elizabeth in her chair beside the radio with the pan of peas that she had been shelling on the floor. With the help of a friend we managed to get her to bed, but she could not understand what had happened or why she was so helpless.

On the 24th of November, 1942, she had a fourth stroke. But with careful nourishment, she was able to make herself understood and could sit up in a chair. And so she lived until April 12th, 1944, when she passed away about ten a.m. from an internal hemorrhage.

ALEXIS C. FERM

APPENDIX B

The Spirit of Freedom

The educator, Pestalozzi, began his work for humanity as a reformer and a revolutionist. After many years of self-sacrifice and struggle he was forced to acknowledge to himself that he had failed to restore the spirit of self-hood in his fellow workman. When he did succeed in kindling any spark of freedom in adults it was only to see it flare up and then die down again. So Pestalozzi finally realized that man, in spite of his desire for freedom was fettered by his past.

But still believing in the law of human development, Pestalozzi turned from the adult to the youth and searched for the clue that would reveal the secret of human progress. He soon discovered that the molding process had imprisoned the soul of youth—that the youth also lacked the spiritual energy to free itself and think and act from within. Undaunted, Pestalozzi turned from Youth to Childhood, trusting to find the evidence of self-expression which he still believed to exist somewhere in human life. In childhood he discovered unrest, opposition, revolt and rebellion, which led him to believe that he was approaching his goal. The vigorous protest of the child against the restraints imposed upon him, which hindered and thwarted the child's self-expression, revealed the fact that a dynamic life force was expressed rebelliously, if not creatively. Pestalozzi believed that he had found a phase in human development free from the static fixed condition of adult life and youth. In spite of the vigorous defiance of the child, Pestalozzi realized that no effort was shown by the child to create a better state or condition in which he could express himself more freely. Instead of being concerned about his own life he found the child arming himself with sticks and stones, forming his gang and marching forth, aggressively attacking everything which reared its head, whether it was human or material.

This reactionary and aggressive tendency in human development, created by adults, brought society face to face with the problem of defense and control. Remedies prescribed,—from Playgrounds to Reformatories,—all of them, in time, revealed their ineffectiveness. The restraint of the inner life of the individual by adults, who assume authority over the young, has and is still the cause of all the violent forms of attack instituted by childhood. As long as we find children playing "Cops and Thieves," "Woolly Woolly, Wolf," etc., we may rest assured that the child has a grievance against adult life which must be eradicated before the child's rebellious attitude will be altered.

Pestalozzi knew that this reactionary state in childhood was not the foundation which he sought; but he was encouraged by it, as a traveller weary and thirsty takes courage to push on in search of a spring after he has come upon a bit of marsh. The marsh indicates that a spring is near.

The violent, reactionary condition of the child against the static, fixed, prescribed rules of adults gave Pestalozzi the impetus to search on for the positive, creative quality in humanity from which would spring a true manifestation of the Spirit of Man and Society.

Pestalozzi concluded that if life was dynamic and free, the simplest manifestation of life must reveal it; so he turned to the infant in his human researches and there he found the assurance after which he was striving. The instinct and impulse for freedom is unmistakably expressed by every child born into the world. Every new born child reveals the impulse as if no restraint had ever been exercised on the human race. It is as persistent and insistent as if there was no law of heredity to influence it.

Pestalozzi's experience was also the experience of his successor Froebel. Froebel based his whole educational work upon a close study of the simple mother with her first-born. Through his mathematical playthings—which he called "Gifts and Occupations," Froebel hoped to aid the child to develop according to the law of the child's own being. Froebel sensitively recoiled from the violent rebelliousness which he too found expressed in the child's activity. He observed the restless activity of childhood and the absence of self-hood in the activity. He rested finally in what he discovered in infancy and realized that he had come in contact with the great fundamental truth of human life.

The infant cannot be intimidated, cannot be reasoned away from his need, cannot be argued away from his demand as long as he is protected by his infant state of consciousness. His consciousness does not include a past or future. He lives in the now, the here. If you enter into a struggle with him he will exhaust everyone of your resources and finally defeat you. His persistency no adult can circumvent. The more you resort to diversion the louder he screams. Nothing is effective but the gratification and satisfaction of his need.

As the infant develops into childhood,—between two and a half and three years of age,—he also develops a mentality which divides his world into two parts, that which includes his home and intimates and the neighborhood life which is distinct and apart from himself. With this development he begins to measure consequences. He sees the reflection of his own acts in the manner toward him of those surrounding him. He begins to realize that if he insists on being himself he must forfeit some material thing as the price. He is warned that unless he submits to one thing and another he must face consequences that he is unwilling to face. Like Esau he finally sells his birthright for a mess of pottage. He discovers that his will and the will of the adult are in opposition. He senses that all grownups have conspired to bend or break him. Self preservation and the gratification of his physical desires suggest that he submit. So day by day we find him getting farther and farther away from the simple natural state of his babyhood where he expressed and revealed the great natural integrity of the universe, entering into a life of concession, compromise and slavery. Instead of finding in grown-ups an understanding that could recognize the crisis through which the child was passing the child finds himself face to face with adults who are as helplessly ignorant as himself of life or the law of human development. The adult consciousness seems to concern itself with things which may be done and things which may not be done, and so the child is hurried and hustled along the path that has been trodden down, and follows the line of the least resistance. The history of his life's progress consists in falling into line and keeping in step with the mass of mankind.

The difficulty even well-intentioned grown-ups experience in dealing with very young children is how to relate the jaded worn-out interests of adult life with the child's natural impulsive spontaneity and persistent self-activity.

If reformers could inaugurate or legislate into existence a perfect social and economic state of Society, we should nevertheless fail to realize any real benefit or permanent change.

A free state—to be permanent—must evolve from a free people. We cannot bestow free conditions. Freedom implies consciousness. We may enjoy a natural condition unconsciously. It is the simple environment of all life, but a free state must be worked for and established consciously. A simple natural state could not be enjoyed by Society today. Grown-ups, who have not expressed themselves self-actively since babyhood would feel awkward and perplexed in a natural condition.

People reared in Cities are affected by the quiet of the country. They are often so affected that they cannot sleep. Close contact with the natural fills them with awe and fear. The lack of diversion—being thrown back on themselves—is too great for them to endure; so they return to the festering human spots, called cities, and feel in the city security and rest because there they have their path laid out for them.

We are often deceived in our relations with adult life by the note of complaint, revolt, or rebellion which adults often express in words. Complaint, revolt and rebellion are indications that the human is dissatisfied with his status and protesting against it. It is no indication, however, that he is in any way conscious of his real need and able to satisfy it. Revolt and rebellion have changed tyrannies, but rarely have they given to man the true foundation for a natural state, not to speak of a free condition. Revolt and Rebellion are tones of protest, they are not in themselves constructive. A free Society, a free condition, would naturally result from a spontaneously self-active, self-employed, self-directing body of humans. It would be the natural expansion of a natural constructive impulse.

Our true economists recognize that any improved social or economic state would have to be carried out and maintained by our children. Our children, consequently, must be educated to live in such a state. It behooves us adults to provide an environment that shall foster the spirit of freedom which the infant has revealed to us. An environment in which he may experience free association with other humans and free access to the material things in that environment. Assured that a natural environment will encourage the expression of natural impulses, the child in time will realize himself as a self-active, self-developing human being. If we succeed in fostering the instinct and impulse of freedom which the infant reveals we may reasonably count on building a free Society.

Southpaw Culture

preserving the public domain
rescuing orphan texts & pirating neglected editions
poetry to politics, pedagogy to planning